D1497969

patty's got a gun

patty's got a gun

Patricia Hearst in 1970s America

William Graebner

THE UNIVERSITY OF CHICAGO PRESS • CHICAGO AND LONDON

William Graebner is the author of *The Age of Doubt: American Thought and Culture in the 1940s*, *Coming of Age in Buffalo: Youth and Authority in the Postwar Era*, and many other books.

The University of Chicago Press, Chicago 60637
The University of Chicago Press, Ltd., London

Printed in the United States of America

16 15 14 13 12 11 10 09 08   1 2 3 4 5

ISBN-13: 978-0-226-30522-6 (cloth)
ISBN-10: 0-226-30522-8 (cloth)

Library of Congress Cataloging-in-Publication Data

Graebner, William.
Patty's got a gun : Patricia Hearst in 1970s America / William Graebner.
p. cm.
Includes bibliographical references and index.
ISBN-13: 978-0-226-30522-6 (cloth : alk. paper)
ISBN-10: 0-226-30522-8 (cloth : alk. paper)
1. Hearst, Patricia, 1954– 2. Hearst, Patricia, 1954– —Public opinion. 3. Hearst, Patricia, 1954– —Trials, litigation, etc. 4. Symbionese Liberation Army. 5. Trials (Robbery)—United States. 6. Kidnapping victims—United States—Biography. 7. Kidnapping—Social aspects—United States—History—20th century. 8. Criminal liability—Social aspects—United States—History—20th century. 9. United States—Social conditions—1960–1980. 10. California—Biography. I. Title.
F866.4.H42G73 2008
364.15'52092—dc22
[B]
2008018320

♾ The paper used in this publication meets the minimum requirements of the American National Standard for Information Sciences—Permanence of Paper for Printed Library Materials, ANSI Z39.48-1992.

For Vanessa and Raluca

contents

figures

Introduction

Patty Hearst's life changed abruptly at 9 p.m., February 4, 1974, when her fiancé, philosophy graduate student Steven Weed, opened the front door of their Berkeley, California, apartment. Two armed men and a woman, members of the Symbionese Liberation Army, pushed their way in. "Bitch," one of them said to Patty, "better be quiet, or we'll blow your head off." In less than three minutes, Patty, wearing only a blue bathrobe, had been gagged, blindfolded, and, her hands bound, dragged through the living room, struck in the face with a rifle butt, and forced into the trunk of a car. She had been kidnapped.[1]

For more than three months following her abduction, Patty Hearst—the nineteen-year-old daughter of Randolph Hearst, son of newspaper tycoon William Randolph Hearst and chairman of the board of directors of the Hearst Corporation—held the attention of the American media, competing for front-page space with the final stages of the Watergate scandal. The SLA released a series of recordings, containing demands and eventually statements by Patty indicating that she now embraced the group's revolutionary agenda. In April, ten weeks after her abduction, she was photographed taking part in the armed robbery of a San Francisco bank. In May the SLA resurfaced in Los Angeles, where six of its members died in a fire following a police standoff. Then Patty and her surviving captors—or comrades—disappeared.

Arrested in San Francisco in September 1975, after more than a year on the lam, Patty again found herself in the spotlight. In January 1976 journalists jammed the U.S. District Court for the opening of her trial for the bank robbery, and her subsequent conviction was, of course, front-page news and the subject of editorial comment in newspapers across the country.[2] Between February 1974 and March 1976, Patty Hearst was on the cover of *Newsweek* seven times.

Given Patty's position as an "heiress" (the noun most frequently used to describe her), her kidnappers' flair for publicity, and some of the bizarre things she did while with the SLA, it was inevitable that she would achieve celebrity status. But one facet of her fame was odd, even discomfiting: Patty was dull. Not dull to a fault, and not dull as in stupid. Just ordinary. Short, moderately attractive, living a "quiet life" of middle-class domesticity in a modest, five-room duplex in a building called "the Townhouse" on Berkeley's Benvenue Avenue, engaged to be married at nineteen. Weed described their lives as "pleasantly routinized with our studies, movies on weekends, laundromat and grocery runs." In summer 1972, at age sixteen, Patty had dutifully set off on a cultural tour of Greece and Italy, only to abandon it halfway through. "I hate to admit it," she wrote Steven, "but I'm terribly homesick. . . . Venice is nice, but smelly. Rome is really beautiful, but I'm afraid to go out of the hotel alone—men don't just whistle here, they run at you and try to grab you! I am even getting tired of looking at all the uncircumcised penises on the statues around here! . . . I may never open another art book again." "The only thing in the world she wanted then," said Weed, "was to have two kids, a collie, and a station wagon."[3]

There was dissonance here. One Patty stood to inherit a portion of the Hearst millions, rode her Arabian horse on the family's eighty-six-thousand-acre estate at San Simeon, swam at the Burlingame Country Club, attended boarding schools, and had been raised by nannies in a twenty-two-room house.[4] Another Patty, the ordinary Patty, lived a simple life. As events unfolded,

Patricia Hearst and her fiancé, Steven Weed, 1973. U.S. Department of Justice, Federal Bureau of Investigation, Record Group 65, National Archives.

a series of new Patty Hearsts surfaced, defined by things Patty did and said and, increasingly, by what people wanted her to do and to be. On an audiotape recorded by the SLA and released March 9, 1974, Patty was an emerging social radical, concerned about race and class and prison conditions, talking about "fascism in America."[5] By mid-April she was a bank robber—caught on film inside a branch of the Hibernia Bank, brandishing a semiautomatic carbine and using the name "Tania," the nom de guerre of the woman who had died in Bolivia while with Cuban revolutionary Che Guevara[6]—and by mid-May she had fired a weapon (actually two of them), spraying bullets at the façade of Mel's Sporting Goods in Los Angeles in an effort to assist her fleeing SLA companions. By the time of her arrest in September 1975, Patty was also a feminist. In the "Tania Interview," written with SLA members Bill and Emily Harris while hiding from the FBI, Patty compared her transformation to the development of a photograph.[7]

The problem of the mutable self is an old one, a product of modernity's disruption of a premodern round of life built on community, tradition, and bedrock expectations about one's life and what one could expect from it. The erosion of those comfortable arrangements brought distress and consternation but also opportunity, perhaps best captured in the nineteenth-century celebration of the "self-made man."[8] A century later, the social upheavals of the 1960s and early 1970s opened up an even greater range of possibilities, all of which were available to an unsuspecting Patty Hearst. In Berkeley, a city symbolic of personal and political change, being an urban guerrilla was a lifestyle option. Race, gender, class, age, sexuality, sexual preference, political commitment, personal appearance, lifestyle—by 1970 all had been unmoored from limits and boundaries and transformed into a smorgasboard of choices. The idea of the "loosening of the self" not only underpinned specific 1970s enthusiasms—for jogging, natural foods, voluntary communities, and the geodesic dome—but also authorized the active search for a new, more "authentic" self, indeed, the very idea of choice. "To be loose," writes sociologist Sam Binkley, "was to choose oneself."[9] By the mid-1970s, the San Francisco Bay Area was home to new movements and organizations offering a variety of nonmainstream ways to "choose oneself": the Peoples Temple, a religious organization that would become infamous for the 1978 mass suicide of its members in Jonestown, Guyana; a powerful lesbian and

Patty, photographed by Steven Weed in front of "La Casa Grande," at her family's San Simeon retreat, summer 1973. Courtesy Steven Weed.

gay community that in 1977 elected the city's first openly gay supervisor, Harvey Milk; Redstockings West and other radical feminist groups; and radical, New Left splinter groups such as Venceremos—and the SLA.

During her trial, images of Patty as an active agent in the creation of her new self came up against her courtroom demeanor, which was passive in the extreme. *Anyone's Daughter*, journalist Shana Alexander's account of the trial, regularly comments on Patty's pasty, gray, "fish's belly" complexion, notes her "copybook plain" handwriting ("as controlled and uninflected as her voice"), and summarizes the court-ordered report on Patty's mental state as describing "a person of 'flat affect' and shallow mind," unusually "concerned with proper hostesslike behavior," a person "living only in the moment, without past or future."[10] The word "zombie" appears frequently in Alexander's account: Patty is "looking totally zombielike once more"; Wendy Yoshimura, her roommate during her year as a fugitive, "saw her as almost a zombie: depressed, withdrawn, subservient"; Dr. Margaret Thaler Singer, one of several court-appointed psychiatrists, labeled the Patty Hearst she observed in October 1975 as "a low-IQ, low-affect zombie"; and a juror later described his confusion in trying to square Patty's dynamic public image with her colorless courtroom visage, "one of them animated, one a zombie." "At the time," this juror recalled, "I couldn't figure out what the hell was going on."[11]

Nor could most Americans. Who was this young woman whose ordinay life and colorless courtroom appearance had been punctuated with nineteen months as captive, bank robber, gunfighter, radical revolutionary, feminist, and fugitive? Was there something extraordinary in Patty's background or makeup that could explain the variety of roles she had taken on in so short a time? Or was this protean Patty a sort of mirror image of the ordinary Patty? And, if that were true, were all ordinary people vulnerable, or open, to such dramatic transformations?

A darker, more threatening explanation for Patty's conduct surfaced frequently during the trial, although, in the end, it did not carry the day. Perhaps the SLA's treatment of Patty—the violent kidnapping, the sexual abuse, the constant threats, the program of indoctrination—had changed something inside her, made her compliant, willing to do anything. Reduced to this state, she resembled others who had been "broken" by their captors and made to do and say things contrary to conscience and character: pilots captured during the Korean War, concentration camp prisoners, and Jozsef Cardinal Mindszenty, a Hungarian prelate who in 1948 penned a "confession" after thirty-nine days of abuse in a Communist prison. In this scenario, Patty hadn't chosen anything, except, perhaps, to stay alive; rather, she was the helpless victim of a powerful new system of mental and physical manipulation.

Was Patty a victim, of duress or fear or what the defense labeled "coercive persuasion," or had she taken up with the SLA willingly, decided to be a different person, chosen a new life? Did Patty's engagement with the SLA have a historical or social cause (the "sixties" and growing "permissiveness" were among the favorites), or was her interior life—that is, her "free will"—sufficient to explain her conduct? If Patty had in some sense been taken over, if she had been brainwashed, turned into a zombie, converted under duress, or otherwise deprived of free will and full consciousness, were other, ordinary Americans, regardless of race, class, gender, and circumstance, just as vulnerable? Should they understand themselves, deep down, as potential victims or as free agents?

At one level these questions were about Patty, about her personality, her identity, and her social being. At another, more fundamental level, they probed the qualities and dimensions of what social scientists called, in the 1950s, the "American character" and, in the 1970s, "human nature." They were also, in the broadest sense, political questions, questions asked of Patty Hearst concerning what had happened to her, but also pertinent to a variety of issues that lay just beneath the surface (and sometimes breached the surface) of everyday affairs—among them the meaning of the 1960s, standards of criminal responsibility, the role of women, and the idea of the welfare state.

These questions had deep resonance for a society caught in a post-Vietnam, post-Watergate climate of malaise, midway between the liberal zeitgeist of the 1960s and the emerging conservatism of the 1980s, between a culture that valued the endurance of the survivor and had compassion for the victim and one that longed for the transcendence of the hero. Patty's ordeal received the attention it did not only because her story was unique and fascinating but because, at the moment of her trial, the most basic issues affecting her guilt or innocence, issues of philosophy and ideology, were unresolved. Had Patty been tried in 1965, she would surely have been acquitted, judged to be nothing more, and nothing less, than the unfortunate victim of kidnapping, rape, and physical and mental torture. Had she been tried in 1985, she would surely have been convicted, steamrolled by the Reagan revolution, judged to be just another person who had failed to take personal responsibility for her acts. The moment of her conviction, in March 1976, was somewhere in between, participating at once in a culture of the victim, grounded in experience and deeply felt, and an incipient culture of personal responsibility. Through most of the trial, attorney F. Lee Bailey presented Patty as victim, gambling that the past would hold, that the future would take its time in arriving. He was wrong.

the story

Abducted

For some time during her captivity, Patty Hearst believed that her abductors were merely one unit in a large and widely dispersed organization. In fact, the Symbionese Liberation Army had just eleven members, and only those involved in Patty's kidnapping were actually "doing" anything. The organization had its origins in 1972 and 1973 in California's Vacaville State Prison, where Donald DeFreeze, one of many inmates committed to a black-power revolutionary ideology, formed close relationships with members of Venceremos, a large San Francisco Bay Area organization whose name derived from the slogan of Castro's Cuban revolution: *Patria o muerte, venceremos!* ("Fatherland or death, we shall triumph!").[1] Venceremos had become deeply involved in the prison movement, and some of its members had formed a prison visitation group that included Willie Wolfe, Bill and Emily Harris, Nancy Ling Perry, Russell Little, and Joseph Remiro. All were convinced that most inmates were political prisoners and victims of economic and social injustice, and all were soon associated with the fledgling SLA.

The SLA presence in Berkeley coalesced in March 1973, when DeFreeze, having escaped from Soledad prison, where he had been transferred, found refuge with Patricia Soltysik and befriended her former lover, Camilla Hall, both of whom joined the SLA. Public consciousness of the organization was heightened in January 1974, when Little and Remiro, their van containing

SLA literature, were arrested and charged with the November 6, 1973, murder of Oakland superintendent of schools Marcus Foster. Black, progressive, talented, and charismatic, Foster had broadened community involvement and persuaded most of his critics that the schools were improving. Nonetheless, for a small number of Bay Area radicals, and some black prison inmates, Foster was "the Black Judas in Oakland," at best an Uncle Tom. Their anger peaked when the school system issued student ID cards. For some, especially black prisoners, the cards betokened a "fascist" police state imposed on black children. DeFreeze made the decision to kill Foster, and the day after the murder the SLA took responsibility for his death in a memorandum delivered to Berkeley radio station KPFA. The organization went underground the same day.[2]

Although SLA contacts with the radical left were numerous, and proved sufficient to shelter the group's members from police and the FBI, the Foster killing proved to be a grave error in judgment, an abomination that set the SLA apart even from militant organizations that might otherwise have been sympathetic to its cause. The Black Panther Party, with its headquarters in Oakland, called the assassination a "brutal and senseless murder," and Weather Underground leader Bernardine Dohrn, while committed to acts of violence and supportive of the Hearst kidnapping, was troubled by the murder. "We do not comprehend the execution of Marcus Foster," she wrote, "and respond very soberly to the death of a black person who is not a recognized enemy of his people."[3]

One imagines that Patty was surprised, if not shocked, to learn that the people who had dragged her down the steps of her apartment and muscled her into the trunk of a waiting car were from backgrounds not that different from her own. While none of the eleven SLA members had been raised by nannies in a twenty-two-room mansion, all but Donald DeFreeze were white and nearly all came from families that were middle class or upper middle class in status and aspiration. (According to a joke making the rounds at the time, membership in the Weather Underground required a credit check on a prospective member's parents.) William Wolfe (whose SLA name was Cujo) was the son of a Pennsylvania anesthesiologist; Wolfe earned average grades at a Massachusetts prep school but was a National Merit Scholarship finalist, with SAT scores in the high 700s. William Harris (Teko), the son of a building supplies salesman, grew up in the wealthy Indianapolis suburb of Carmel, where as a youth he attended services at St. Christopher's Episcopal Church and played on the high school golf team. Emily Harris, née Schwartz (Yolanda), was raised in affluent, suburban Clarendon Hills, Illinois, where her father was an engineering consultant. Bill and Emily met at Indiana University, where he pledged Sigma Alpha Epsilon fraternity and Emily, a stylish, straight-A student, joined the Chi Omega sorority, serving as its social chairperson.[4] The oldest of the SLA women at twenty-nine, poet and painter Camilla Hall (Gabi) was the daughter of a Lutheran minister in the prosperous Chicago suburb of Lincolnwood and a humanities graduate of the University of Minnesota. Patricia "Mizmoon" Soltysik (Zoya), the daughter of a pharmacist, was an honors student at a Goleta, California, high school before enrolling at Berkeley, where she and Hall became lovers. Nancy Ling Perry (Fahizah) was the daughter of Hal Ling, who operated Ling's Furniture in Santa Rosa, California, and was active in local politics as a Goldwater conservative. At Montgomery High School, the cute, four-foot-eleven Perry was a cheerleader and class secretary. She attended Whittier College before transferring to Berkeley.[5] The origins of Angela Atwood (Gelina) were similarly modest, though not insubstantial. She grew up in a small, all-white town in New Jersey, where her widowed father was business manager for a Teamsters local. Angela's zeal for high school academics and extracurricular activities—cheerleading, student council, honors society, Catholic Youth Organization—reflected middle-class aspirations to upward mobility. As with the Harrises, her next stop was Indiana University.[6] Like Patty, at least

The six SLA members killed in the May 1974 fire at the group's Los Angeles safe house. Top, from left: Camilla Hall, 29; William Wolfe, 23; Donald DeFreeze, 30. Bottom, from left: Angela Atwood, 25; Nancy Ling Perry, 26; Patricia Soltysik, 29. AP/Wide World Photos.

five members of the SLA had traveled in Europe. Most, write Vin McLellan and Paul Avery in their history of the organization, "had rejected a great deal."[7]

Donald DeFreeze—black and not of middle-class origins—was the great exception. Born in Cleveland in 1943 and raised in the city's black ghetto, Donald was the oldest of eight children. At age fourteen, he left an abusive father for Buffalo, New York, where he boarded with a Baptist minister and took some solace in religion. Before long, however, he found himself in trouble with the law for auto theft and was sent to the reformatory at

Elmira, where he stayed for two and a half years. DeFreeze was subsequently arrested on weapons charges in East Orange, New Jersey, and again in Los Angeles in 1965. His gun-related criminal activities continued, though by 1967 he was also apparently working as a small-time informer for the Los Angeles Police Department. In 1969 he was convicted of armed robbery and sent to Vacaville State Prison.[8]

From the beginning, the press mocked the SLA's ideology and methods and professed to be unable to figure out what the organization stood for or wanted. "The SLA had no real program," opined the *Charlotte Observer*, "no clear vision of a different world." Anticipating the "rebel without a cause" analysis that would emerge during the trial, the *Richmond News Leader* editorialized, "If SLA members had a Cause, it was difficult to define from the half-baked rhetoric periodically issued from SLA hideouts."[9]

There's no denying the half-baked (or overcooked) quality of the SLA's rhetoric. Its missives usually ended with "Death to the Fascist Insect That Preys upon the Life of the People," a tagline that captured the group's violent, extremist populism, as well as its lack of subtlety. Yet the SLA did have its causes and concerns, and most would have found a sympathetic hearing within the liberal community. Among them were the nation's criminal justice and prison system; urban poverty and malnutrition; the widespread exploitation and oppression of the poor, blacks, Hispanics, women, and servants; and, unusual though hardly unprecedented, the sense that ordinary people had been conditioned by the public schools and drugged by materialistic consumer affluence into uncritical acceptance of their circumstances. Writing to her parents just days before the Hearst kidnapping, Emily Harris charged them with complicity in perpetuating the suffering, poverty, and dead-end jobs that constituted the lot of most people. "These realities," she insisted, "exist because some people insist on being rich regardless of whether they must utilize the blood and sweat of others. . . . I will never be free until there are no more rich people and no more poor people. This means that I can no longer relate to the aspirations you have for creating a comfortable life for yourselves because they ignore the tortured lives that others lead in an attempt to survive." No less important, Emily and the other SLA women had strong feminist views opposed to restrictive female roles and middle-class standards of beauty, dress, and sexual conduct, tolerating but chafing under the sexist tyranny of DeFreeze and the macho swaggering of Bill Harris.[10]

The ideological superstructure of the SLA was Marxist and Maoist, the latter derived from the association of Wolfe, Little, Perry, and DeFreeze with Peking House, a North Oakland, communal living space where a Maoist perspective—emphasizing military strategy and activism, along with the "reeducation" of those deemed to have wrong ideas, rather than class-based organizing—prevailed, and where the SLA took shape in the summer and fall of 1973. SLA members read books and followed world events and were especially well informed about third world revolutionary movements, including those in the Philippines, Mozambique, and Puerto Rico. References to the "ruling class" and the "fascist capitalist class," denunciations of capitalist exploitation, injunctions to class warfare, and calls for armed revolution abound in the SLA literature. The group's white, middle-class membership, tormented by racial guilt and in awe of blacks' courage in defying oppression, embraced militant strategies of resistance based on armed violence and, some would add, terrorism: bank robbery, kidnapping, and, with the murder of Marcus Foster, assassination.[11]

Within an hour of her kidnapping, Patty had been transported to a "safe house" on Northridge Drive in Daly City, a suburb just south of San Francisco, and put in a small, smelly closet (twenty-five by seventy-nine inches), padded but otherwise empty, where she would remain for about six weeks, the first two weeks blindfolded, the first few days without access to a toilet. Disoriented and frightened, Patty was briefly reminded of Barbara Jane Mackle, a kidnap victim who in 1968 had been put in a box and buried. According to her testimony, for a few seconds Patty thought that she too was being buried alive. In her first hours in captivity, Patty met DeFreeze, who introduced himself as "General Field Marshall of the Symbionese Liberation Army." While in prison for armed robbery, he had taken the name Cinque Mtume, the first name that of the leader of the 1839 revolt on the slave ship *Amistad*, the last name derived from the Swahili word for "prophet." Cinque threatened Patty with death if she tried to escape, and with being beaten or hung from the ceiling if she made noise. He informed her that she was a prisoner of the SLA, which she recognized as the organization that had claimed responsibility for killing Marcus Foster. She was told that, as a prisoner of war, her treatment would be consistent with that meted out to SLA members Remiro and Little, who were being held in San Quentin as suspects in the Foster murder.[12]

In the hours and days that followed, Cinque, Gelina (Angela Atwood), and others lectured Patty at length on the SLA's deep interest in prisons and victimized prison inmates, the SLA "Codes of War," the role of the SLA's "guerrilla fighters" in bringing about the revolution, and other aspects of the organization's worldview. Day 3 brought the beginning of what Patty called "interrogation," a hostile, accusatory inquiry into Patty's "bourgeois" family past, including Randolph Hearst's finances and family connections, culminating in Cinque's decision to use the daughter to force the father to spend his millions to feed the state's poor. The food program—eventually called People in Need—was developed on Day 5, when Cinque and Patty, together in Patty's closet, made the first of several audiotapes, which would be released to the public on February 12. On it, Patty assured her parents that she was "okay" and "not being starved or beaten or unnecessarily frightened." Cinque explained that Patty's "arrest" was for "crimes that her mother and father have committed against we the American people and the oppressed people of the world." Without offering Patty's release, he called for a "token gesture" from the Hearsts: the distribution of seventy dollars' worth of food to each of hundreds of thousands of poor people in thirteen California communities, a demand that, fully implemented, could have cost four hundred million dollars. After the taping, with Patty exhausted and in tears, and still blindfolded, Cinque fondled her breasts, pinched her nipples, and "grabbed my crotch," communicating what Patty later described as "the threat of sexual violence." She concluded that the attack might have been brought on by remarks she had made to Zoya (Patricia Soltysik) the previous day, expressing concern that her life would be in danger if the poor refused to accept food purchased with "blood money."[13]

As the days went by, the indoctrination continued. Patty sat against the back of the closet while, outside, Cinque, Gelina, Zoya, or someone else read newspaper clippings about "revolutionary 'actions'" in places like Puerto Rico or the Philippines, expounded on the SLA's "opinions and theories," or condemned Patty's previous way of life as "bourgeois and sexist." In *Every Secret Thing*, her 1982 memoir, Patty recalls thinking that most of this was "pure nonsense." Nonetheless, the experience made her realize that she had been remarkably "sheltered" from issues of politics and foreign affairs. During this period of reeducation, she also had time to consider her situation and to ponder the possibility of her release. Difficulties in implementing the food-distribution program perhaps added to her anxiety. "I mostly thought," she testified at her trial, "that I would be killed."[14]

If one can believe Patty's account, the epiphany she experienced sometime in late February or early March entailed, not a guilty recognition of her bourgeois values or her place in the class structure, but a renewed determination to live. "I decided that I would not die," she recalled, "not of my own accord. I would fight with everything in my power to survive, to see this through. . . . I decided I would not think of the future. I would concentrate on staying alive one day at a time." In the sixth week of her 1976 trial, a key prosecution witness, Joel Fort, would claim that by

March 1, roughly the time Patty would claim she had committed herself to staying alive, Patty had joined the SLA, voluntarily.[15]

Patty's recollection of the next few weeks suggests some of the strategies she used to survive as a prisoner of the SLA. She absorbed the ongoing efforts at her reeducation with something like passive resignation, learning that the food program, as her father had agreed to it, was a "mockery"; that the symbolic bombings carried out by the Weather Underground made them "phony revolutionaries"; that Marxist activist Angela Davis was "a pig who had betrayed" George Jackson, a black prisoner killed in 1971 during an escape attempt and a legendary figure for the radical left; that a vote for Nixon was better than a vote for McGovern, because the latter's social reformism muddled the issues and confused the masses; and that she was likely to be killed if there were an FBI raid. Something may have changed inside her too. "I accommodated my thoughts to coincide with theirs," she recalled. "I had lived in fear of the SLA for so long now that fear of the FBI came easily to me."[16]

Patty also "accommodated" herself to the sexual desire of two SLA men. Her concession, if that was indeed what it was, was consistent with the obligation, apparently recognized by all the group's members, that SLA women satisfy the sexual "needs" of their male comrades. Although the women were all committed feminists, and hence aware that servicing the "macho" men was somehow retrograde, the group's focus on military survival skills in the weeks following the kidnapping left feminist values in abeyance. "Without realizing it," recalled a document written by Patty and Emily Harris more than a year later, "our concept of what a female guerrilla should be was *male defined*." Patty's first encounter with this aspect of the SLA took place in mid-March, the day after Cinque first broached the possibility that she might be permitted to join the organization. "You can join us and fight with us," he told her, "or you can die." The next day Cujo (William Wolfe) went into the closet and, as Patty recalled, "did his thing and left." Sex with Cinque took place in the following week and was doubly obligatory. To have sex with the SLA leader was deemed an honor, and because Cinque was black, to reject him would have been viewed as racist. This round was as perfunctory as the last. "I lay there like a rag doll," Patty recalled, "my mind a million miles away. It was all so mechanical and then it was over. I said to myself, rationalizing again, 'Well, you're still alive.'"[17]

Cinque's tentative offer to let Patty join the SLA became firm a week or ten days later, almost immediately after the group left Daly City for a new safe house, on Golden Gate Avenue in San Francisco—with a new, even smaller closet for Patty. According to Patty, the choice Cinque had earlier presented remained implicit, and so she said yes: "I want to join you." Cinque followed up: "That'll mean, you know, you never can go back to your old way of life. You'll be an urban guerrilla, fighting for the people." Patty's reply was swift. "Yes," she said. "I want to fight for the people." She was momentarily flushed with a curious sort of happiness, grounded in relief. "All I could think about," she recalled, "was that I would live." In the eighth week of her trial, prosecution witness Dr. Harry Kozol would claim that Patty had voluntarily joined the SLA "some weeks" before the bank robbery, around or before the first of April—quite possibly before she made a formal commitment to the organization.[18]

Of course, the public could not have known of Patty's "decision," nor much else about her state of mind as these events were taking place. Its knowledge was limited to a series of audiotapes released by the SLA and to whatever the press learned from Patty's parents and friends about how she might be expected to be dealing with her situation. Despite this dearth of information, in early April, following the release of the fifth tape, on which Patty affirmed her commitment to the SLA and its values, the public began to turn against her or, alternatively, to conclude that she was under such extraordinary duress that she now believed, in some way, in the SLA credo—that she had been "brainwashed." The first sign that Patty was losing favor came from the *Arizona*

Not long after Patty "agreed" to join the Symbionese Liberation Army, she posed for this photograph, wearing Fahizah's beret and wielding a sawed-off M-1 rifle, with the SLA flag as a backdrop. The rifle scope was only for effect; it was tied on. Patty's hair was cut immediately after the photo was taken. The details come from Patricia Hearst's book, *Every Secret Thing*. U.S. Department of Justice, Federal Bureau of Investigation, Record Group 65, National Archives.

Republic, whose editors decided that the threat of terrorism posed by the SLA, which it saw as part of an international movement, rendered moot the question of Patty's mindset. Without committing to one explanation or the other for Patty's statements on the latest tape, the *Republic* coldly pronounced "the issue of Patty Hearst settled—no matter how horrible it must be to her family." Patty's parents were stunned. After hearing the tape, Randolph Hearst refused to believe that Patty had joined the SLA. "We've had her 20 years, they've had her 60 days, and

I don't believe she's going to change her philosophy that quickly or that radically." "I know my girl," added Patty's mother, Catherine Hearst, a political conservative who had served for many years on the Board of Regents of the University of California. "She would never join any organization like that without being coerced." Steven Weed, who spent a lot of time with the Hearst family in the weeks after the kidnapping, wrote that "what really burdened Catherine was the shame and disgrace of it all. The disgrace, particularly the disgrace!" In contrast, San Francisco television reporter John Lester, who became the spokesman for the family in the days after the kidnapping, describes Randolph and Catherine handling the experience with dignity, decorum, humor—and more than an occasional scotch.[19]

For a time, the Hearsts found common ground with most of the press—and presumably much of the public—which rallied behind the ill-defined idea of brainwashing, acknowledging some sort of mental change or conversion but deeming it involuntary. Randolph Hearst had been shaken by his daughter's comments on the sixth tape, delivered in early June to Los Angeles radio station KPFK, on which Patty had said she would "never choose to live the rest of my life surrounded by pigs like the Hearsts." After listening to the tape at the family's Hillsborough home, he had said, "Well, she really talked herself into a shot in the ear. It sure looks like her conversion is complete. I think she's so far gone she'll never come back." The *Montgomery* (Alabama) *Advertiser*, while suggesting that Patty "may have had a prior disposition toward the revolutionary philosophy of her captors," speculated that the SLA had brought out that disposition through "subtle conditioning, involving reward and punishment." *Today*, a publication of the *Chicago American*, found evidence of brainwashing in the dead, mechanized quality of Patty's voice, indicative of a person "who can no longer make rational choices."[20]

At this point, before Hibernia and before Mel's, investigating authorities had not yet decided whether Patty was staying with the SLA of her own volition. By late May, that position had changed. According to the Los Angeles district attorney, who filed felony charges against Patty for participation in two kidnappings in the hours after the incident at Mel's, "Miss Hearst was acting on her own free will. . . . She is a suspect in a kidnapping, not a victim." He admitted, however, that he had never before heard of a case in which a kidnap victim had become a kidnap suspect.[21]

Whether or not Patty's decision to join the SLA was voluntary, events now moved rapidly toward her rendezvous with the Hibernia Bank. Within a week, Patty had been liberated from the closet, her hair had been cut short, and she had confirmed to Cinque that she had not been "brainwashed." She had also recorded a portion of the SLA's fifth tape (received April 3 at radio station KSAN), denying that she had ever "been forced to say anything on tape" or "been brainwashed, drugged, tortured, hypnotized, [or] in any way confused," an apparent response to speculation in the press that one or all of those things had occurred. Once the upcoming bank job had been announced within the SLA, Patty was photographed for publicity purposes with a sawed-off M-1 rifle and issued a similar gun that was to be her own. Increasingly treated as a member of the group, she was introduced to her revolutionary name, Tania, and—a shock to her middle-class sensibilities—to the communal toothbrush. In an apparent gesture of friendship, Willie Wolfe (Cujo) presented Patty with a rope necklace featuring a small stone charm that he described as "his most treasured possession," a twenty-five-hundred-year-old Olmec monkey. The ensuing days were packed with weapons instruction and elaborate physical combat drills, all conducted, for security purposes, in the tiny apartment.[22]

The Robbery

On April 15, cameras inside the branch of the Hibernia Bank at Noriega and Twenty-second streets in San Francisco captured Patty Hearst with a shoulder-strapped carbine—perhaps loaded and ready to fire, perhaps not—pointed at bank employees. She was ringed by SLA comrades, whose guns, Patty's defense would argue, were trained on her. In the course of the robbery, Patty was to make a short speech, one that would convince the public that Patty Hearst was there, robbing a bank, and that she hadn't been brainwashed. Frightened and perhaps confused, she managed to blurt out, "This is Tania . . . Patricia Hearst," but nothing more. The day after the robbery, a San Francisco home owner took down a sign that had been prominently displayed since the kidnapping. It read, "God Bless You, Patty."[23]

Had testimony in her trial been limited to the events prior to and including the robbery of the Hibernia Bank, Patty might well have been acquitted. She had made some incriminating and inflammatory statements on the SLA tapes, and she had been in the bank with a weapon. But at this point, the popular presumption—not shared by the U.S. attorney general or many others—was still that her words and deeds were those of a kidnap victim acting out of fear and under duress. Instead, the jury was allowed to learn of an incident that occurred about a month after the robbery at a Los Angeles sporting goods store.

One of many photos taken by cameras inside the Sunset Branch of the Hibernia Bank in San Francisco, April 15, 1974. William Harris is at left, Patricia Hearst at right. U.S. Department of Justice, Federal Bureau of Investigation, Record Group 65, National Archives.

On May 8 or 9, with the heat on in the Bay Area and about ten thousand dollars in its coffers from the bank heist, the SLA moved its operations to a safe house in Los Angeles, located on West Eighty-fourth Street in Compton's black ghetto. Cinque had divided the group into "combat units," and in the week after the move, Patty drilled with her unit—consisting of herself, Teko, and Yolanda (that is, Bill and Emily Harris)—while Cinque drank plum wine, acted out the part of an abusive drill sergeant, and announced that he was a "prophet." On the afternoon of May 16, Patty's combat unit, suitably disguised (Patty was wearing an Afro wig and blue horn-rim glasses), went shopping. Their third stop was at Mel's Sporting Goods on Crenshaw Boulevard. Yolanda parked their VW van in a shopping center lot across

Patricia Hearst, wearing a wig, in the Hibernia Bank. It is not clear whether Patty's gun was loaded or, if it were, whether she knew it. U.S. Department of Justice, Federal Bureau of Investigation, Record Group 65, National Archives.

the six-lane street, and she and Teko went inside. Tania read the newspaper and waited. Beside her, on the floor of the van, were a handgun, an automatic carbine, a semiautomatic carbine, and a 12-gauge shotgun—all loaded.[24]

Tania looked up to see Teko struggling on the ground outside the store with several men—store employees, she would later learn, one of whom had observed him shoplifting an inexpensive shoulder cartridge belt. Yolanda was being held too. In her 1982 account, Patty recalled her reaction. "I could see both Teko and Yolanda looking over in my direction. They were staring right at me, waiting for me to take action. I immediately knew what to do. I had been trained and drilled in this very combat maneuver over and over again." She grabbed the automatic carbine, shoved its sawed-off barrel out the driver's side window, and opened fire. Twice the weapon jumped from her hands, but within seconds she had emptied the thirty-shot banana clip, hitting the bushes and the concrete barrier that divided Crenshaw and spraying Mel's façade. When that weapon was exhausted, she picked up her own semiautomatic carbine and fired three more shots to her left, striking a light pole, as the Harrises, now free in the chaos, ran across the street.[25]

On the stand, under cross-examination, Patty would describe her response as a "reflex action" produced by her SLA weapons and combat training, akin, she would later argue, to that of "Pavlov's salivating dog." "It happened so fast, I just didn't even think about it." When the prosecuting attorney argued that her response consisted of two, separate actions—firing the first gun, then picking up a second and firing that—Patty insisted that they were aspects of a single, unitary response: "It all happened in a matter of seconds, the whole thing of the firing and picking up the other gun even. . . . It was all part of the response that we were supposed to have when something like that happened." "By the time they had finished with me," she concluded in *Every Secret Thing*, "I was, in fact, a soldier in the Symbionese Liberation Army." With the Harrises on board and the van screeching out of the parking lot, Tania turned to Teko and asked, "Did I do right?" He replied angrily, "What the fuck took you so long?"[26]

Reluctant to return to the Eighty-Fourth Street safe house, the team drove the streets of Los Angeles for hours in four stolen vehicles, waiting for a preplanned rendezvous with their

Mel's Sporting Goods on Crenshaw Boulevard in Los Angeles, ca. 1975. The photograph was taken from roughly the spot where Patty opened fire on May 16, 1974, riddling the façade with bullets, apparently in an attempt to assist Bill Harris, who was struggling with a store employee. Russ Reed/*Oakland Tribune*.

comrades that would never take place. One of the vehicles belonged to eighteen-year-old Thomas Matthews, who was snatched along with his Ford Econoline, only to be introduced to a "smiling" Tania. Matthews's testimony would prove damaging. Patty, he recalled, insisted that she had entered the Hibernia Bank with a functioning carbine; said SLA weapons had not been trained on her during the robbery; and, alone with Matthews for a short period, stated that she had "changed her views." And she had *not* asked him to get a message to her parents.[27]

The Fire

Late the next afternoon, in a motel room near Disneyland, Teko turned on the television to discover that more than a hundred police officers had surrounded what they said was an SLA safe house on East Fifty-fourth Street in Los Angeles. The Mel's incident had made the previous quarters untenable, and Cinque and the others had relocated to a site unknown to Patty's team. As they watched, it became clear that neither the police nor area residents knew whether Patty was one of those trapped inside. When the SLA refused to surrender, police fired tear gas grenades into the structure and a shootout began. Somehow, the small stucco house caught fire (the police would claim that a gas can inside the house had been struck by a bullet). Another call for surrender was answered with more gunfire. Within minutes, every occupant of the house—Gelina, Gabi, Fahizah, Zoya, Cujo, and Cinque—was dead. Deeply troubled by what she had seen, Patty reflected on what could have been her fate. "I knew that if I had been in there," she later wrote, "the police would have behaved precisely the same way. Why would they do anything else? Cin[que] had told me it would be that way. If I had been there, I would be dead now." Patty locked herself in the bathroom. "I sat there on the floor in a stupor. I was a soldier, an urban guerrilla, in the people's army. It was a role I had accepted in exchange for my very life. There was no turning back. The

May 17, 1974. Following an hour-long gun battle between police and members of the SLA, the group's south-central Los Angeles "safe house" went up in flames, killing everyone inside—including, some believed at the time, Patricia Hearst. In fact, Patty watched the event on television at a motel, with Bill and Emily Harris. AP/Wide World Photos.

police or the FBI would shoot me on sight, just as they had killed my comrades."[28]

Patty's reaction was justified, and not just because of the devastation she had seen on television (which had, indeed, taken place without the authorities' knowing whether Patty was inside). In mid-February, about two weeks after the kidnapping, U.S. attorney general William B. Saxbe, a former senator and a member of the Ohio National Guard unit that had fired on student antiwar protestors at Kent State University in 1970, had implied that the FBI would be right to risk a shootout—and Patty's life—if it knew the location of the SLA. Under attack from the Hearst family and the press for the remark, Saxbe had backed off, saying the FBI would take no action that would put Patty in jeopardy.[29] Then on April 17, two days after the Hibernia robbery, Saxbe had again said something that would have made Patty question her safety. "The entire group [the SLA]," he announced, "is common criminals," adding—on nothing more than a hunch—"and Miss Hearst is part of it." Although the press for the most part saw the remark as insensitive, unnecessary, and irresponsible, for Patty it would have been just another sign that Saxbe and his FBI could not be trusted.[30]

On the morning of May 27, Memorial Day, Teko, Yolanda, and Tania, the sole surviving "combat team," left Los Angeles and headed north, beginning a sixteen-month journey that would take them across the country and back. Much, but not all, of what came to be known as the "missing year," they spent together. Patty was arrested by the FBI on September 18, 1975, in San Francisco, where she was living with Wendy Yoshimura, an associate of Bill, Emily, and Patty during much of the missing year, and one of the founders of the SLA women's collective. William and Emily Harris were arrested the same day at their apartment, a few blocks away.[31]

Early Reactions

In the days and weeks after Patty Hearst was taken away in the trunk of a car, Americans struggled to interpret the event, to understand the SLA and its actions: the abduction, the murder of Marcus Foster, the demand for money to feed the poor, and Patty's appearance at the Hibernia Bank. Many of the following early editorial responses predate the robbery, and most predate Patty's trial by more than a year.

Given the common belief that terrorism on American soil is a recent development, with its roots in the 1993 bombing of the World Trade Center, it may surprise some to learn that the Hearst kidnapping was widely, although not universally, interpreted as an act of terrorism, and not an isolated one at that. One school of thought saw the kidnapping as part of a worldwide proliferation of terrorism that included actions by the Irish Republican Army, Uruguay's Tupamaros, the Palestinians, and Libyan leader Moammar Qaddafi, whom the *Arizona Republic* suspected of financing the SLA with oil money.[32] "By 1974," wrote Jay Cantor, looking back from the early 1980s, "one's hopefulness at an end—terror had become, it seemed, the substance of 'revolutionary' politics. If you wanted to participate you had to be ready to pick up this gun, become a terrorist; ready to sacrifice others, sacrifice yourself."[33]

By late May 1974, a week after the Los Angeles fire that killed six members of the SLA, the *Emporia Gazette* wrote that knowledge of how Patty had decided to join the SLA would shed light on terrorism in the Golan Heights, Ireland, and Munich, the last shorthand for the Arab murder of Israeli athletes at the 1972 Olympic Games. According to this story line, terrorism had at one time been restricted to "over there" but was now, rather suddenly it seemed, "over here." "We can no longer look down our noses at the small and violent states in which it has long been a fact of life," the *Daily Oklahoman* announced. "Terror has come to our own streets and neighborhoods." The attorney general of the United States, William B. Saxbe, pushed the SLA link to foreign terrorism even further. Interviewed in early April, Saxbe claimed that Patty Hearst's abduction closely followed instructions laid out in a Maoist manual, and that the existence of the manual pointed to a "worldwide conspiracy" responsible for the Hearst kidnapping as well as others conducted in the months that followed.[34]

Others were more likely to see SLA terrorism as homegrown. Writing for the *Los Angeles Times*, UCLA political science professor David C. Rapoport traced what he called the "terrorist mystique" to the Weathermen, a militant spin-off of Students for a Democratic Society, and to the post–Civil War version of the Ku Klux Klan. A year later, following Patty's arrest, the Portland *Oregonian* described her "terrorist kidnapers" as the product of "violence-prone eggheads, drug users and sex-obsessed misfits of the nation who want to 'save' America by murder, arson and elimination of its leaders to 'destroy the system'" (somehow neglecting to indict rock n' roll). The *Arkansas Democrat* at least had the courage to name names, implying that Angela Davis, Jane Fonda, Huey Newton, and radical lawyer William Kunstler, by "openly advocating violence and even practicing a little of it themselves," had contributed to a climate conducive to terrorism. The *Daily Oklahoman* argued that terrorist activity had emerged on college campuses because of the presence there of "illicit drug traffic," which, so the argument went, encouraged radical groups to "maintain their intense feelings of hatred for others."[35]

Anxiety about terrorism also contributed to the complex public reaction to the People in Need food giveaway, funded by six million dollars extorted from Randolph Hearst (all but five hundred thousand dollars of which was provided by the Hearst Foundation and the Hearst Corporation; apparently Randolph's personal resources were much more limited than the SLA, or the public, had thought). As carried out, the program had a serious side but also a farcical one. On the one hand, thousands of bags of groceries were distributed in the Bay Area in February and March 1974. On the other hand, not all of the food reached the hands of those most in need—at one point, a twenty-thousand-dollar truckload of canned hams disappeared. Even when it did, the positive impact was short-term, and given California's estimated 4.7 million poor and needy, the Hearst money amounted to little more than a dollar per person. Worse, the February distribution was marred by violence: at a distribution center in Oakland, thirteen thousand people mobbed delivery trucks; one woman lost an eye in the chaos, and many more were treated in hospital emergency rooms.[36]

Like Hurricane Katrina in 2005, the SLA demand brought increased visibility to the poor, and with it, controversy. The Baltimore *Afro-American* welcomed the heightened public consciousness of poverty, contrasting policies that sent billions of dollars to Vietnam and Israel for weapons with the new evidence that the nation contained so many people "not living the 'American Dream.'" On the other end of the political spectrum, the *Indianapolis Star* cataloged all the money then being spent on supposed "victims," characterized the food program as a dangerous experiment in "share-the-wealth" economics, and suggested that the SLA assist the "real poor" by fighting against Russian and Chinese communism. Although the *Star* never explicitly denied that the U.S. poor existed—indeed, it insisted that the nation's gross national product, evenly distributed, would not make much of a dent in the poverty problem—in March 1974 it repeated a story by reporters from the *Village Voice* claiming that the "needy" were mostly men in "wide-brimmed velvet hats" and women with "bouffant hair-dos," who arrived to pick up their free SLA groceries in Cadillacs, Mercedes, and Lincoln Continentals. California's governor, Ronald Reagan, accused those who accepted the food of "aiding and betting lawlessness" and, speaking at a Republic luncheon, said, "It's just too bad we can't have an epidemic of botulism."[37]

Both right and left seemed to agree that the SLA's demands had put the poor in a position of moral responsibility, perhaps even on the front line of the battle against terrorism. At the very least, the poor were expected to weigh their need for the proffered food against the repugnant circumstances that had made it available. Indeed, in mid-February, before plans were finalized and food actually distributed, there were reports that some potential recipients would draw the line at accepting aid from kidnappers. Newspapers noted signs that the poor were too proud and too ethical to participate in the SLA's sordid scheme; according to the *Emporia Gazette*, two relief clients, for example, not only had rejected any future benefit but had contributed an amount equal to the value of the food to a fund for the release of Patty Hearst. Those who saw the nation as being on the slippery slope of terrorism fervently hoped that the poor would take a stand against the food program. "So this burden, too, as if their needs were not burden enough, has fallen to the poor," wrote the *Dayton Daily News*. Without dismissing the idea that the kidnappers had revealed unseemly aspects of American social life, the *Wichita Eagle* insisted that the solution was wrong and that the poor should deliver the message: "The rejection of food at the potential price of Patricia Hearst's life by all who would be eligible for the extorted supplies under guidelines set by the SLA, could only be interpreted as mass rejection of terrorism as a means of correcting whatever social inequities may exist in America."[38] That proved to be a fantasy. The poor showed up and took the food.

Regardless of whether the SLA was explicitly referred to as "terrorist," its deeds, and to a lesser extent, Patty's, were often presented as a product and example of 1960s and early-1970s radicalism. Some admirers of the era's radical efflorescence might have agreed and embraced the SLA, while others would have denounced the SLA's means, if not its ends, and contested the association with what they regarded as a period of admirable action (the Black Panthers and Weather Underground had, indeed, condemned the murder of Marcus Foster). But for many commentators references to the sixties were clearly (and at times strategically) pejorative, intended to discredit simultaneously a group known for kidnapping a coed, murdering a school official, and robbing a bank—if that were necessary—and the decade and its legacy. Describing a "sense of déjà vu," the *Wall Street Journal* found in the SLA's rhetoric of "liberation" and the "ruling class" echoes of earlier manifestos by the SDS, the Revolutionary Youth Movement, and the Black Panthers, documents "celebrated by the radical chic"—meaning, apparently, white liberals who should have known better.[39] The "anti-sixties," as historian Philip Jenkins describes the period starting in 1975, had begun.[40]

A different critique of 1960s liberals came from the *Dallas Morning News*, which interpreted the Hearst kidnapping as "another of the grim products of the old 'direct action' fad. " "The core of that fad," the paper explained, "was the claim that breaking the law in the name of a political cause makes the act political rather than criminal." While that definition would include college students sitting in at segregated lunch counters, antiwar activists pouring blood on draft files, even Rosa Parks refusing to give up her seat on a Montgomery bus, the paper argued that through such action, legitimate dissent became simple terrorism: the "nail bomb set off in a public place," "the murder or maiming or kidnapping of some citizen." Similarly, the *Birmingham News* claimed that political kidnappings of the Hearst variety (such as the February 1974 abduction of J. Reginald Murphy, editor of the *Atlanta Constitution*, by an opponent of the Vietnam War) were the product of years of police restraint and tolerance of sixties-style street demonstrations. The *Charlotte Observer* acknowledged that protests against the Vietnam War had been reasonable and valuable but linked the SLA to a rhetorical, polemical, and ineffectual streak of 1960s protest, comparing the organization to "those forlorn college students of several years ago who saw the purchase of velour bellbottom trousers as a revolutionary act."[41]

Patty's image as coed heiress made it difficult, but not impossible, for the press to reconstruct her as a child of the 1960s. These efforts grew more common after the receipt of the fifth and sixth SLA tapes, on April 3 and April 24, 1974. On the former, Patty denied that she had been "brainwashed" or drugged and announced that she had come to embrace a universal love, the cause of "freedom of all oppressed people," and a political perspective that held the "corporate state" responsible for the energy crisis, unemployment, and other ills. On the April 24 tape, Patty said she had participated in the Hibernia robbery voluntarily, called her family the "pig Hearsts" and Steven Weed a "sexist, ageist pig," and concluded by describing herself as "a soldier in the People's army."[42]

Following the release of the fifth tape, the *Winston-Salem Journal* concluded that Patty had perhaps never been "the sweet young San Francisco socialite she has been made to appear." Rather, the paper reported, she had told her father that his newspaper was "an irrelevant rag geared to senior citizens," been dismissed from school for smoking pot (a charge that was never confirmed), and spent too much time with boyfriend Steven Weed—a "leftist graduate of Princeton," where he had "roomed with a black militant and a member of the SDS." Writing in September 1975, after Patty's arrest, *Chicago Sun-Times* columnist Bob Greene labeled Patty Hearst and the SLA as anachronisms, pathetic holdovers from the 1960s, when "the dramatics, the histrionics, the threats and slogans" might have been taken more seriously. At that same juncture the *Dayton Daily News* wondered how Patty and the Harrises had managed to hide for so long, and suggested that the rugged Western terrain that had hidden 1930s bank robbers Clyde Barrow and Pretty Boy Floyd had given way to social "canyons" on the "new frontier in extremes." Patty's most recent predecessors, the *News* wrote, were the strange and sometimes dangerous children of the sixties: "The Mansonettes, seeking flower-child summers but finding themselves as mass murderers, raiding lives as if they were plunder. Political rabbit holes from which fallen PhD candidates emerge as Weathermen. Pitiful bands of Jesus freaks, lost on behalf of a God who must cry for the waste."[43]

More than a little of this child-of-the-sixties rhetoric would emerge at the trial. The prosecution found it convenient, and hoped it would prove persuasive, to ground Patty's actions in the recent past, to see her as just the latest in a succession of misguided souls. "I think this was all *in* her," Dr. Harry Kozol would testify. "In a sense, she was a member of the SLA in spirit, without knowing it, for a long, long time."[44] But there was something else going on. Although the SLA/Patty Hearst "event" was the *immediate* object of media and public interest in the mid-1970s, for those critical of the political left there were bigger fish to fry. The biggest of those fish was an alternative politics—represented by the New Left, the civil rights movement, the counterculture, feminism, and even Great Society liberalism—that remained a genuine, albeit flagging, challenge to the nascent free-market, family-values consensus that would emerge full-blown under Reagan. To link the SLA with the movements of the 1960s, then, was to associate the left/liberal politics of the decade with an organization identified as irresponsible, extreme, dangerous, and terrorist.

The most common response to the Hearst kidnapping and subsequent events, and perhaps the most comforting one for Americans troubled by signs of social change and upheaval, was, however, to *unmoor* Patty and the SLA from any concrete, radical historical precedents—the Black Panthers, the prison movement, the New Left, the counterculture, Jane Fonda, the

Manson family—and to trivialize and marginalize their behavior and to frame their conduct in ways that denied the political content of their actions. Most of these efforts tapped into a growing hostility to the youth-oriented social movements of the 1960s, and most used psychological concepts and analyses to explain why neither the SLA nor Patty Hearst deserved to be taken seriously.

Topping the list was "permissiveness," a term that repackaged undesirable conduct as the product of a society and institutions that were—in the past or at present—irresponsibly lenient and lacking in discipline, especially toward the young and wayward (rather than, say, toward corporate polluters). In the late 1960s and early 1970s, the word was usually associated with the child-rearing ideas of Dr. Benjamin Spock, whose *Common Sense Book of Baby and Child Care* had sold millions of copies since its publication in 1946. The charge that Spock's advocacy of permissive child-rearing methods was responsible for the turmoil of the 1960s first surfaced in 1968, when the Rev. Norman Vincent Peale asserted that parents' adoption of those methods had resulted in "the most undisciplined age in history." Nixon's vice president, Spiro Agnew, who detested the New Left and the counterculture, made a similar accusation in 1970.[45] An apparent epidemic of teen use of the drug PCP, or "angel dust," was the focus of a powerful, panic-driven assault on permissiveness in 1976, followed in 1977 by another panic, this time over child abuse and sex crimes—again, predictably, blamed on the permissive sixties.[46]

According to the press, different sorts of permissiveness were responsible for the SLA/Hearst debacle. William Loeb, publisher of the *Manchester Union Leader*, surveyed the criminal record of Donald DeFreeze, lamenting that the SLA leader had first gone to jail only after his tenth offense. Loeb argued that if the courts had handled DeFreeze more "firmly," rather than dropping charges for parking meter theft, weapons possession, and other crimes, the Hearst kidnapping might never have happened. Looking more broadly at a recent rash of kidnappings and hijackings, the *Roanoke Times* claimed that the frequency of such crimes was a product of a criminal justice system that punished rarely and lightly. Making the right-wing thrust of these arguments more explicit, the *St. Louis Globe-Democrat* blamed "liberals in Congress" for a surge in terrorism that included the Hearst kidnapping, identifying "today's climate of permissiveness" with a series of liberal positions, including opposition to the death penalty, wiretapping, FBI surveillance, the House Un-American Activities Committee, and a 1971 Nixon proposal for a new law on terrorism. In a March 1974 speech calling for reinstatement of the death penalty in certain kidnapping cases, Nixon cited the Hearst incident.[47]

Another target was the college campus. Attempting to explain what had brought the white, middle-class members of the SLA to "declare war on American society," the *Richmond News Leader* looked to the University of California at Berkeley, known since the Free Speech Movement of 1964 as a hotbed of student activism, and to what it described as that campus's "atmosphere for radical behavior." "Fungus thrives in humid warmth," the paper elaborated. "Perhaps violence thrives in the vacuum of permissiveness that exists on some campuses these days." For *Boston Globe* columnist Jeremiah V. Murphy, Bill and Emily Harris were typical of a generation of young people from well-to-do families who had been given license to "do their own thing" in the heyday of Vietnam protests, the "Age of Anything Goes." "Suddenly there weren't any rules any more," wrote Murphy, "and the kids almost ran some colleges, because otherwise there would be a strike, and the professor passed too many students who didn't look at a book or otherwise those same students would flunk out and would be drafted. Nobody wanted to have that happen." Permissiveness reigned supreme. Bill and Emily Harris turned "sullen" and "unhappy," then crossed the line into violence and terrorism, and eventually found themselves in jail.[48]

Patty had never paid much attention to politics—"Steve and I," she wrote, "heard of no protests, knew no radicals"—and the phrase "anything goes" hardly captures her round of life in the Berkeley community, where she studied for classes, worked as a clerk at Capwell's Department Store in Oakland, went to the movies, enjoyed the cafes and bookstores, watched TV, and did her laundry at the Wash House. Nor does "permissiveness" do justice to what Patty describes as a childhood policed by a "strict," anxious, and "overprotective" mother who insisted on curfews and prohibited slumber parties and blue jeans. "We were not spoiled," she wrote in 1982, "nor did I ever sense that I was being overindulged."[49]

Even so, the Hearst millions left Patty vulnerable to the charge that she was the proverbial "spoiled rich kid" whose early indulgence had blossomed into high defiance. She was the "wayward child with affluent parents," a "rebellious miscreant," one of those "provocatively naughty children in skilfull [*sic*] adult bodies."[50] In the fall of 1975, when Patty shared the front pages with would-be assassins Lynette "Squeaky" Fromme and Sara Jane Moore, the *Indianapolis News* focused on Patty's money and the indulgence it implied to link her to two women who had tried to kill the president. "Born to affluence and culture," Patty had been indulged. She had received eight thousand dollars on her eighteenth birthday and a monthly allowance of three hundred dollars while living with Weed, "all the while dabbling in revolutionary nothingness." In the media spectacle that was Patty and Squeaky and Sara, Americans were, said the *News*, "reaping a harvest of shame—the inevitable denouement to a generation of youth worship, permissive parenthood, and soft-headed justice."[51]

Permissiveness, then—permissive parents, permissive campuses, permissive liberals, a permissive system of criminal justice—was one framework within which the curious SLA/Patty Hearst phenomenon could be understood as beyond politics, or at least beyond a politics that grew out of basic social and economic conditions—race and gender relations, poverty, prison conditions, and the like. The other route to avoiding the unsettling conclusion that Patty and the SLA actually *meant* something, or stood for legitimate social concerns, was to talk and write about them as if they were mentally unstable or otherwise pathological. The protagonists, all of whom (with the possible exception of Patty) believed in what they were doing, resisted any such identification; neither Patty nor the Harrises would claim insanity as a defense, and the Harrises are known to have bristled at press speculation that Cinque's death in the Los Angeles fire was a suicide.[52]

Pathology has been used often, and effectively, to marginalize political and social dissidents. In the years immediately following World War II, Hollywood films frequently featured strong women—women who were making social statements—resolving personal "problems" through Freudian therapy. The Warren Commission interpreted Lee Harvey Oswald's assassination of John F. Kennedy, a political act linked to American efforts to kill Fidel Castro, as the deed of a bitter, alienated man whose life had been a failure. And Daniel Patrick Moynihan, looking back in *The Moynihan Report* (1965) on decades of protest by black Americans against discrimination and poverty, argued that the source of their discontent was not white racism or joblessness or urban renewal—all matters that had political remedies—but African American "family pathology."[53]

The press did something similar, but less refined, to the SLA. The *Wall Street Journal* set the tone on the tenth day after Patty's abduction, suggesting that the "grievances" of the SLA (the quotation marks are those of the *Journal*), expressed in its demand that food be distributed to the poor, "seem to be an exploitation of the poor in the pursuit of murky and sinister psychological urges." The *Kansas City Times* compared the SLA to the Ku Klux Klan, though to which of its incarnations—1870s, 1920s, or 1950s—was unclear. "Psychologically all the pieces fit," noted the *Times*—the "paranoia, the messianic posturing," the "childish fascination with queer names and elaborate symbols"; SLA members were, in a word, "sick." The accusation of infantilism also appeared in the *Richmond News Leader*, which belittled the SLA's theories, with their "Marxist trappings," as "childish imaginings of a make-believe world—little girls and boys playing dress-up in mommy's and daddy's clothes." Other newspapers discovered in Cinque's SLA a Hitlerian schizophrenia, an alienated neuroticism, or similarities to the bloodthirsty Manson family.[54] Cinque was labeled a "mad dog," and the Los Angeles County coroner, astounded that none of the victims of the May 17 fire had tried to escape, ordered a "psychological autopsy" to discover what had motivated these six "determined fanatics."[55]

The events of September 1975—the arrests of Patty, Squeaky Fromme, and Sara Jane Moore (who was reportedly obsessed with Patty), and the bombing of a Seattle supermarket in retaliation for Heart's arrest—brought a new round of comments about "crazies," "psychos," "the madness of alienation," and, referring to the SLA, "mentally sick people."[56] A reporter for the *Sacramento Bee*, covering Patty's arraignment, drew a curious lesson from the diminutive stature of Patty, Wendy Yoshimura, and the Harrises, none of whom, she wrote, were much over Patty's five-foot-three. "A giant of a crime story," concluded Victoria Graham, "was thus reduced to a brief appearance by four short, slight people in a quiet courtroom, an altogether incongruous climax to the thunder and passion of the Symbionese Liberation Army." Although by this time it was widely accepted that Patty had joined the organization, the press did not explicitly include her among the deeply disturbed. Columnist Bob Greene went as far as anyone in labeling her a "crazy little girl," but to him it meant misguided and mildly deluded, not psychotic. Nonetheless, the comment functioned to separate Patty from whatever serious political or social motives she may have had for joining and remaining a member of the SLA.[57]

The Missing Year

For sixteen months after the Los Angeles fire that killed most of the members of the SLA, the "crazy little girl" had avoided an FBI dragnet. Patty had taken on yet another name, Pearl, and she recalls "frequent mix-ups with names at this time. . . . I responded to the name Tania or Patty and tried to grow accustomed to answering to my new code name, Pearl, which I did not like much." With Bill and Emily Harris, Patty traveled first to Berkeley, where the trio made contact with Jack Scott. Until then best known as a sports activist who had supported the African American sprinters who raised gloved hands in a "black power" salute while receiving their medals at the 1968 Olympic Games, Scott, the self-proclaimed "Harriet Tubman" of the radical underground, arranged to drive the three fugitives across the country to a rented farmhouse northeast of Scranton, Pennsylvania. Patty, wearing horn-rim glasses and a wig (SLA members often wore disguises), made the journey in a Ford LTD with Scott and his parents and without the weapons she was by now accustomed to carrying. The remnants of the SLA were joined in Pennsylvania by Wendy Yoshimura, who belonged to the Revolutionary Army, which had carried out bombings in northern California to protest the Vietnam War. An art student, Yoshimura had been born in a Japanese internment center and raised in what remained of Hiroshima. She and Patty, who shared an intense dislike of the Harrises as well as

NATIONAL FIREARMS ACT

William Taylor Harris

Date photographs taken unknown
FBI No.: 308,668 L5
Aliases: Mike Andrews, Richard Frank Dennis, William Kinder, Jonathan Maris, Jonathan Mark Salamone, Teko
Age: 30, born January 22, 1945, Fort Sill, Oklahoma (not supported by birth records)
Height: 5'7" **Eyes:** Hazel
Weight: 145 pounds **Complexion:** Medium
Build: Medium **Race:** White
Hair: Brown, short **Nationality:** American
Occupation: Postal clerk
Remarks: Reportedly wears Fu Manchu type mustache, may wear glasses, upper right center tooth may be chipped, reportedly jogs, swims and rides bicycle for exercise, was last seen wearing army type boots and dark jacket
Social Security Numbers Used: 315-46-2467; 553-27-8400; 359-48-5467
Fingerprint Classification: 20 L 1 At 12 / S 1 Ut

Emily Montague Harris

Date photographs taken unknown
FBI No.: 325,804 L2
Aliases: Mrs. William Taylor Harris, Mary Hensley, Joanne James, Anna Lindenberg, Cynthia Sue Mankins, Dorothy Ann Petri, Emily Montague Schwartz, Mary Schwartz, Yolanda
Age: 28, born February 11, 1947, Baltimore, Maryland (not supported by birth records)
Height: 5'3" **Eyes:** Blue
Weight: 115 pounds **Complexion:** Fair
Build: Small **Race:** White
Hair: Blonde **Nationality:** American
Occupations: Secretary, teacher
Remarks: Hair may be worn one inch below ear level, may wear glasses or contact lenses; reportedly has partial upper plate, pierced ears, is a natural food fadist, exercises by jogging, swimming and bicycle riding, usually wears slacks or street length dresses, was last seen wearing jeans and waist length shiny black leather coat; may wear wigs
Social Security Numbers Used: 327-42-2356; 429-42-8000

NATIONAL FIREARMS ACT; BANK ROBBERY

Patricia Campbell Hearst

FBI No.: 325,805 L10
Aliases: Tania, Susan
Age: 21, born February 20, 19[illegible], San Francisco, California
Height: 5'3" **Eyes:** Brown
Weight: 110 pounds **Complexion:** Fair
Build: Small **Race:** White
Hair: Light brown, may be dyed blonde and cut short **Nationality:** American
Scars and Marks: Mole on lower right corner of mouth, scar near right ankle
Remarks: Hair naturally light brown, straight and worn about three inches below shoulders in length, however, may wear wigs, including Afro style, dark brown of medium length; was last seen wearing black sweater, plaid slacks, brown hiking boots and carrying a knife in her belt

Feb., 1972

Dec., 1973

April, 1974

(artist conception) Summer 1974

THE ABOVE INDIVIDUALS ARE SELF-PROCLAIMED MEMBERS OF THE SYMBIONESE LIBERATION ARMY AND REPORTEDLY HAVE BEEN IN POSSESSION OF NUMEROUS FIREARMS INCLUDING AUTOMATIC WEAPONS. WILLIAM HARRIS AND PATRICIA HEARST ALLEGEDLY HAVE USED GUNS TO AVOID ARREST. ALL THREE SHOULD BE CONSIDERED ARMED AND VERY DANGEROUS.

Federal warrants were issued on May 20, 1974, at Los Angeles, California, charging the Harrises and Hearst with violation of the National Firearms Act. Hearst was also indicted by a Federal Grand Jury on June 6, 1974, at San Francisco, California, for bank robbery and use of a weapon during a felony.

IF YOU HAVE ANY INFORMATION CONCERNING THESE PERSONS, PLEASE NOTIFY ME OR CONTACT YOUR LOCAL FBI OFFICE, THE TELEPHONE NUMBER OF WHICH APPEARS ON THE FIRST PAGE OF MOST LOCAL DIRECTORIES.

C M Kelley
DIRECTOR
FEDERAL BUREAU OF INVESTIGATION
UNITED STATES DEPARTMENT OF JUSTICE
WASHINGTON, D. C. 20535
TELEPHONE: 202 324-3000

Entered NCIC
Wanted Flyer 475 AA
(Rev. April 10, 1975)

The FBI issued a wanted poster soon after the Hibernia robbery. The first poster described Hearst as a "material witness." This revised version, from April 1975, identifies Patricia Hearst as a "self-proclaimed" member of the SLA and describes her, William Harris, and Emily Harris as "armed and very dangerous."

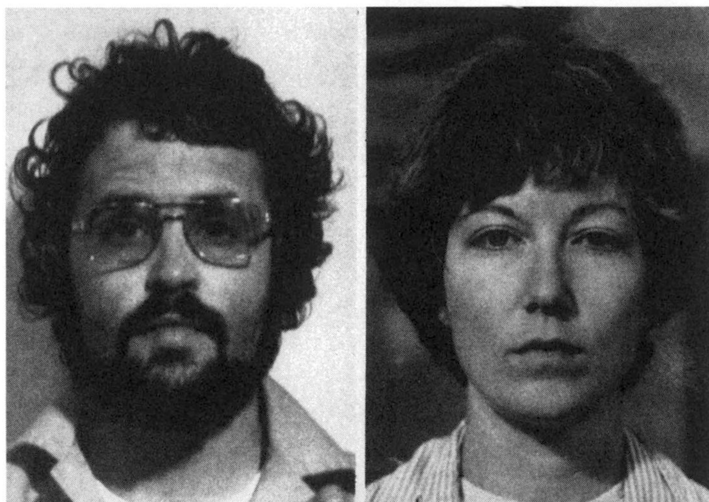

Police identification photos of William and Emily Harris, taken following their capture in San Francisco, September 18, 1975. *Buffalo Courier-Express* Collection, Buffalo State College, Archives and Special Collections.

an interest in art, became friends. "This quiet and wise woman," Patty wrote, "opened my mind to horizons somewhat broader than those of the SLA."[58]

While in Pennsylvania, and later at an abandoned dairy farm in southern New York State, the SLA cohort (Yoshimura was not a member) drilled with weapons, conducted grueling physical conditioning exercises, and worked on what was envisioned as a book about the SLA. Leaked to the press when Patty was captured and, in a controversial ruling, made available to the jury, the manuscript comprised a series of interviews. Patty's twenty-seven-page portion became known as the "Tania Interview." In it, Patty tore into her parents with vituperation and specificity, at one point narrating a family visit to Catherine's hometown, Atlanta, where her mother had explained the absence of signage in black neighborhoods with the comment "Niggers don't need street signs." Patty presented her conversion to the SLA as a matter of education in a new, idealistic set of values, describing her transformation from heiress to "freedom fighter" as a "process of development, much the same as a photograph is developed." Claims that she had been brainwashed represented "cheap sensationalism." "If you believe the media you'd think that I was totally weird. Acccording to them, I never mean anything I say, and I'll do anything I'm told." Although the defense would ask the jury to dismiss the "Tania Interview" as coerced propaganda, journalist Shana Alexander, observing in the courtroom, felt that those pages resonated with the tapes to bring Tania to life. "The manuscript," she wrote, "means that Tania exists or, at least, that she once did."[59]

In mid-September 1974 the cadre moved back to the West Coast, settling in Sacramento, where, joined by other political radicals, they planned and executed two more bank robberies. Patty was involved in only one of them; she drove the "switch car" for the April 1975 robbery of the Crocker National Bank in Carmichael, a Sacramento suburb, during which a woman was killed. Reviled by the Harrises as an unworthy comrade and fearful of being caught, Patty was miserable. "My hair was growing longer," she recalled, "but it was also falling out in great clumps. My nails were chewed down beyond my fingertips. I chain-smoked all day long and fidgeted in nervous anxiety." She cried frequently.[60]

The Arrest

Seeking relief from the intense Sacramento manhunt, the group, now including Berkeley radicals Kathy and Steve Soliah and Jim Kilgore, moved to San Francisco in May 1975, eventually settling in several safe houses, one occupied by the Harrises, another, at 625 Morse Street, by Patty, Wendy Yoshimura, and Steve Soliah.[61] Patty gave gun classes for the women in the group and took part in women's studies sessions, discussing the place of women in the revolution while pouring over Shulamith Firestone's book *The Dialectic of Sex*. In August Patty helped plan and bring off the bombing of an empty police car at the Emeryville police station, across the bay from San Francisco. Overall, her mood remained bleak. "I was trapped in this nether land of radicals and revolutionaries," she later wrote. "Theirs was the only world I had. I did not really know what I believed anymore. It did not seem to make much difference. There were telephones all over the city but calling someone was beyond me. I was troubled and anxiety-ridden, for it seemed that even without the Harrises, I could find no mental peace." On September 18 the Harrises were arrested while jogging near their apartment. An hour later, the FBI and San Francisco police, working with information provided by the Soliahs' father, surprised Patty and Wendy at their Morse Street apartment. Special Agent Tom Padden saw Yoshimura, then Patty, rising from the kitchen table. Leveling his .38, he yelled "FBI . . . Freeze." Moving through

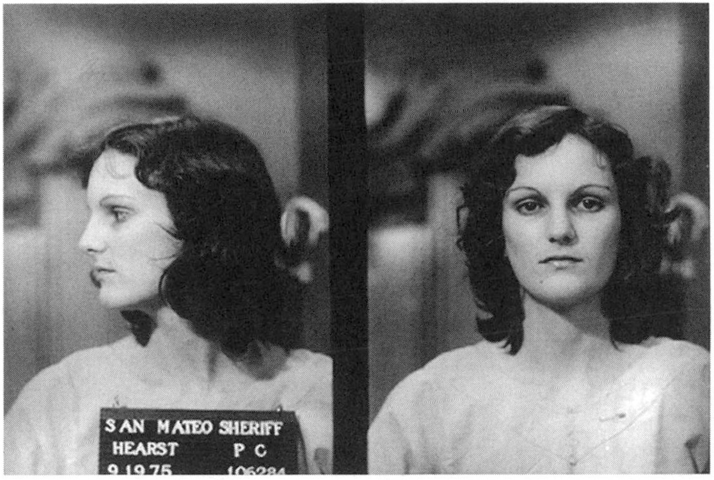

Identification photo of Patricia Hearst, taken at the San Mateo County Jail, September 18, 1975.

the room toward a retreating Patty, police inspector Tim Casey called out, "Patty!" and then, "Don't move!" "She looked pale and scared," Casey remembered. "I went over and put the cuffs on her. She didn't give any trouble." The owner of the building, who had followed the officers up the back stairs, recalled that as Patty turned around in response to Casey's commands, she "laughed, then giggled, then put her hands up." Minutes later, as Padden was gathering the group to leave, Patty politely asked if she could change her clothes; she had wet her pants. When informed of her daughter's arrest, Catherine Hearst said, "Thank God she's all right," then, to the press, "Please call it a rescue, not a capture."[62]

The tone of malaise, introspection, and anxiety with which Patty, in her 1982 book, colored her last months with the SLA contrasts, at times sharply, with the circumstances surrounding her capture and with her conduct in the hours and days that followed. Several details stand out. When arrested, the government revealed a day later, Patty had a loaded .38-caliber pistol in her purse, and two rifles were found in a closet. Her first stop,

Patty Hearst, shortly after her arrest in San Francisco, September 18, 1975. AP/Wide World Photos.

apparently, was at FBI headquarters at San Francisco's Federal Building, where, in a slowing automobile surrounded by reporters and photographers, Patty "smiled broadly and raised a clenched fist in salute." "I had a role to play and I knew my part well," Patty recalled.[63]

At her arraignment in federal court late that afternoon, on charges of bank robbery and firearms violations, Patty appeared defiantly casual. Some of that was unavoidable; she was wearing the plain rubber sandals and brown corduroys in which she had been captured, with no socks and no bra. But she had chosen to wear tinted sunglasses, to chew gum, and, according to the *New York Times*, to swing her hips. "She looked carefree and relaxed," commented the *Times*. "And she smiled a lot." From the counsel table, according to UPI reporter Jack V. Fox, "she turned once to the spectator section and gave a closed fist salute." Hours later, at the San Mateo County Jail, she was again in character. Asked for her "occupation" for the jail records, Patty first replied that she had no job, then, when the deputy insisted, answered, in words that would appear in every daily newspaper, "urban guerrilla."[64]

More revealing, perhaps, was a conversation that took place two days later, still at the jail, between Patty and a visitor, lifelong friend Trish Tobin. Apparently, Emily Harris was in the visitors' room too, perhaps within earshot. Unaware that the conversation was being taped—and that the jury would hear its contents—Patty told Trish that "my politics are real different from way back when," and that once out on bail she planned to make a statement, from "a revolutionary feminist perspective." When Trish reported that Catherine Hearst was overjoyed that Patty had been found, Patty replied rather coldly, "I was so pissed off, Goddamn it." Nor did the prospect of rejoining her mother and father appeal to Patty, who feared she would be "a prisoner in my parents' home."[65]

Patty's arrest brought to the fore two other issues, each of which would influence the outcome of her trial. One was the issue of social class, reframed and made more intense by the prospect, now imminent, of a rich girl at the bar of justice. The other, at once inevitable and, given the near-simultaneous arrests of Patty, Squeaky Fromme, and Sara Jane Moore, fortuitous, was the issue of the woman with a gun. After nineteen months with the SLA, Patty knew a lot about guns—enough, at least, to break down and reassemble every weapon in the SLA arsenal and to instruct others in their use—and the bullet-riddled façade of Mel's Sporting Goods proved that the young woman was not afraid to pull the trigger—or triggers. Janey Jimenez, the U.S. marshall who, unarmed, escorted Patty after her arrest, recalled that "she knew more about guns than I did. She said to me, 'You know, you ought to have a gun.'"[66] During the trial, the prosecution presented Patty as a woman who had grown comfortable with guns, emphasizing how she had demonstrated familiarity with the M-1 to the kidnapped Thomas Matthews in the aftermath of the incident at Mel's, and pointing out that when arrested, her purse held a fully loaded Smith & Wesson handgun.[67]

Gun-toting Patty had her counterparts in the popular culture. Shana Alexander tells the story of Summer Robin Bartholomew, Miss USA in 1975, who, dressed in combat fatigues and sporting a real automatic rifle, carried out a simulated stickup at the opening ceremonies of the Miss Universe Contest in San Salvador. Ms. Bartholomew, Patty Hearst, or, indeed, any of the women of the SLA could have inspired the screen persona of Lt. Ellen Ripley (played by Sigourney Weaver), the tough, competent, monster-killing heroine in the 1979 movie *Alien*.[68]

But public perception of Patty Hearst was more profoundly shaped by Squeaky Fromme and Sara Jane Moore, women with guns who shared the front page in September 1975, both charged with attempting to assassinate President Gerald Ford. The red-haired Fromme, twenty-six, had grown up middle class in Santa Monica, California; become a member of Charles Manson's notorious "family"; and on September 5 had gone after Ford, one of five thousand "earth polluters" marked for death by her paper organization, the International People's Court of Retribution.[69]

Moore, a forty-five-year-old veteran of five marriages and the mother of four children, shot at the president on September 22, dressed in men's clothing. Also from a middle-class background, Moore had abandoned a suburban, country-club lifestyle and a career as a CPA to work with Bay Area radicals, write for the leftist *Berkeley Barb*, and, from time to time, serve as a paid informant of the FBI. Unlike Fromme, Moore had ties to Patty Hearst and her family. After Patty was abducted, Moore had helped the FBI investigate "Tom," an SLA sympathizer who had two friends killed in the Los Angeles shootout and fire, and she had been an early volunteer for the SLA food-distribution program. When her role as an FBI informant was publicly revealed in June 1975, Moore, increasingly sympathetic to the goals of the SLA, took up the cause of locating Patty Hearst. The arrests of Patty and the other SLA fugitives brought an end to that ambition, and Moore shifted her attention to killing the president. Explaining her act to a reporter for the *Los Angeles Times*, she said that she hoped it would galvanize the radical movement to "forge some kind of unity between the rage that led to the formation of the SLA combined with the theoreticians."[70]

It was a juicy story with a lot of angles, and it would have touched Patty even if Moore had not been entangled in the activities of the SLA. In a *Chicago Sun-Times* article (titled "Women with a Gun") that did not mention Patty, experts agreed that the new wave of female violent crime was a sign not of genuine liberation but of women's inability to control their lives or to deal with increased independence. Nor was Patty mentioned in another story that labeled Fromme and Moore "deranged California markswomen," though she must have come to mind for many readers. The *Indianapolis News* made the connection explicit, referring on its editorial page to the "latest volcano of nihilism" that had "erupted" in the "Patty Hearst–Squeaky Fromme–Sarah [*sic*] Moore spectacle." And liberal syndicated columnist Georgie Anne Geyer suggested that Fromme and Hearst were among the "least 'liberated'" of women. Patty was also tarred, perhaps inadvertently, by newspaper layouts that juxtaposed stories on the Hearst defense's request for psychiatric examinations and on the psychiatric tests that Moore was undergoing, and that, in at least one case, put stories about Patty, Sara, and Squeaky in close proximity on the front page.[71]

As historian Laura Browder suggests in a recent book, Patty's use of guns and identification with the SLA brought her into a frame occupied by Weather Underground member Susan Stern, Black Panther activist Assata Shakur, and other threatening women who, in the 1960s and 1970s, advocated revolutionary violence against the state or in the cause of women's liberation. This, in turn, made Patty's trial "a public forum on the cultural meanings of women's revolutionary violence." But because the SLA's political ideology could be easily dismissed, Browder argues, the media generally lumped Patty instead with the 1930s gangster Bonnie Parker and the Manson girls, inviting readers to see her as the bizarre product of a highly sexualized feminism run amok, and her attraction to phallic weaponry as an expression of an energizing, but deeply disturbing, "sexual awakening." "Patty Hearst," concludes Browder, "embodied a cultural nightmare about the violent potential inherent in all women and about the power of promiscuous sex to unleash that violence."[72]

Patty's change in status from fugitive to defendant also brought renewed emphasis, and a new slant, to the subject of class. To be sure, this was not the first time issues of class had surfaced in the Patty Hearst drama. In Patty's apparent rejection of her previously comfortable circumstances, some had detected a disturbing trend that threatened to undermine the assumptions of the affluent society. The SLA's demand that Hearst money be used to feed California's hungry had momentarily brought attention to the existence of the poor and, more troubling, had broached the always controversial solution of redistributing income. Yet neither issue achieved anything like the universal acceptance that greeted the latest idea about class, namely that money must not determine the outcome of the trial.

This idea had great appeal because it seemed so right, so obviously valid: there must not be "one law for the poor and another for the rich," as the *Chicago Daily Defender* put the issue. The handling of the Patty Hearst case would thus measure the fairness of the American system of justice. Yet beneath the ostensible consensus swirled disparate currents of politics and social interest; everyone espoused the cause of equal justice before the law, but for a variety of reasons. For liberals, the hope was that Hearst family money would not bring the judicial system into disrepute, or so distort the legal process that valuable social lessons would go unlearned. *Newsday* downplayed Patty's transgressions, depicting her as "an unlikely candidate for anyone's chamber of horrors," and suggested that the "relentless" search for a young woman guilty of "baffling misadventures" had served largely to place the FBI and the White House among "other recently disinflated institutions." Patty's trial, then, would determine whether the justice system also joined the "disinflated." The *Chicago Sun-Times*, concerned that Patty's conversion to urban guerrilla might presage a larger social upheaval among the nation's youth, hoped that the Hearst wealth would not prevent the legal proceedings from shedding light on the central question of the susceptibility of the young to complete and rapid changes in values. A reporter for the same newspaper uncovered a very different perspective while interviewing blacks in the Los Angeles neighborhood where, in May 1974, most of the SLA had died. "That White girl ain't going to do time," a man named Melvin said. "Shoot, baby, that's what being rich people is about. You watch what I'm saying."[73] In his speech accepting the Democratic nomination for president in the summer of 1976, Jimmy Carter echoed the antielitism of the time. "Too many," he said, "have had to suffer at the hands of a political and economic elite who have shaped decisions and never had to account for mistakes, nor to suffer from injustice."[74]

To the right of center, especially, expressions of support for equal justice under the law masked a growing conviction that Patty was guilty, and that a guilty verdict would be rendered unless the Hearst fortune thwarted the process. In Columbia, South Carolina, *The State* called for proceedings untainted by money and influence, for an evenhanded process that would belie the "widespread belief in this country that there are two standards of justice—one for the rich, one for the poor." This and other commentaries alluded to an underlying moral narrative grounded in the family: though probably not innocent—she was, after all, charged with serious crimes and so far had not explained how she could have failed to escape during the "missing year"—the "prodigal daughter" might be forgiven. Expressions of this argument emphasized Patty's relationship to her parents. The *Charleston Gazette*, for instance, referred to "the film showing Mrs. Hearst's little darling standing in a bank lobby and cradling a submachine gun during a stickup," and the Springfield, Massachusetts, *Union*—not so obviously on the right—to how Randolph Hearst's parental hopes were mocked by Patty's "clenched fist salute." Nonetheless, if the trial proceeded in "normal fashion"—that is, if the power and influence of the Hearsts were held at bay—Patty would go to jail.[75]

The Trial

Opening arguments in the trial of Patty Hearst took place in U.S. District Court for the Northern District of California on February 4, 1976, two years to the day after she was kidnapped. The 170-seat, nineteenth-floor, high-security courtroom was packed with journalists and the few members of the public lucky enough to get in. The presiding judge, sixty-four-year-old Oliver J. Carter, a graduate of Stanford University and Hastings College of Law, had a folksy manner but also a sharp tongue and a decided impatience with arguments whose validity he doubted. He had already decided that Patty could not be trusted with bail, that a jury composed mostly of people who had knowledge of the Mel's incident and other events in Los Angeles could be a reasonable one, and that his own relationship with the Hearst family, limited but going back many years, would not affect his judgment.[76] On this day, in response to a request that the prosecution be prohibited from bringing up in its opening statement certain events and time periods (Mel's, the missing year) that had not yet been ruled relevant to the indictment, Carter replied, "I understand what you are saying, Mr. Bailey. As we say upcountry, you can't unring a bell." Mr. Bailey was quick with his retort: "You can't get a skunk out of a courtroom once you bring it in."[77]

"Mr. Bailey" was celebrity attorney F. Lee Bailey, the head of Patty's legal team. At age forty-three, Bailey was coming off triumphs in several high-profile cases, including the court-martial of Captain Ernest Medina for involvement in the My Lai massacre in Vietnam; the trial of the "Boston Strangler"; and the retrial of Dr. Samuel Shephard, accused of murdering his wife (and the basis for the popular television series *The Fugitive*). Bailey was known for his expensive clothes, his tough cross-examinations, and his fondness for the media; in 1970, he had been censured by a Massachusetts judge for "extreme egocentricity." Patty's other attorney was J. Albert "Al" Johnson. Johnson lacked Bailey's flamboyance, but he knew more about Patty than anyone else, having spent hundreds of hours with her in the jail. The prosecution was led by U.S. Attorney James R. Browning Jr., also forty-three, a Nixon appointee and former president of the Young Republicans, who lacked recent trial experience but not brains. Johnson's counterpart on the government team was David P. Bancroft, thirty-eight, described by Shana Alexander as "a jut-jawed, Ivy League barracuda." The prosecution team also included Edward P. Davis Jr., a recent graduate of Santa Clara University Law School and, in 1973–1974, law clerk for Judge Carter.[78]

The opening statements by Browning and Bailey laid out arguments and revealed perspectives that would have resonance for the jury when it deliberated six weeks later. Within the first minute, Browning had placed Patty Hearst at the robbery of the Sunset branch of the Hibernia Bank; within three minutes he had presented the jury with a diagram showing the bank's location and another showing its interior and explained the operation of the bank's surveillance cameras ("four frames per second"), in preparation for narrating the robbery and Patricia Hearst's part in it. It was all about the bank. Then, surprisingly, Browning introduced the jury to the events at Mel's Sporting Goods and to Patty's gunplay there. When Browning finished, Bailey moved immediately for a mistrial on the grounds that the latter information "taints that jury so it no longer can hear this case." Judge Carter denied the motion. A few days later, in a ruling even more prejudicial to Patty's defense, he would rule that all of Patty's statements made after the bank robbery had been made voluntarily.[79]

In his opening statement, Bailey told a very different story, one that began with the assassination of Marcus Foster by SLA "terrorists" and moved quickly to the kidnapping, sexual assault, and psychological terrorizing of a young, "apolitical" woman living a "most ordinary life." Bailey's story culminated not in the Hibernia robbery or in the incident at Mel's (which went unmentioned), but in the Los Angeles fire that killed most of the SLA and made the FBI and the federal government into objects of Patty's fear. The purpose of his story was not to contest what Patty had or had not done, but to offer a view into the "mind control" methods of the SLA and, especially, into Patty's state of mind. The jury heard that a "foreign army," the SLA, had "brainwashed" Patty—described as a "prisoner of war for 20 months"—with techniques similar to those applied by the Chinese to POWs during the Korean War. While still in the closet, Bailey argued, her "will" had been "broke[n]." "Her terror was real." The Patty inside the Hibernia Bank, the Patty who did not try to escape, was a creature lacking in will, no longer in control of her actions: a victim. The proof, Bailey concluded, would come from the testimony of psychiatrists and other experts on thought reform and brainwashing.[80]

Patty took the stand, for the first time in the presence of the jury, nine days later, on the afternoon of Friday, February 13. She was wearing a gray flannel pantsuit and an apricot silk shirt, but smart clothes could not mask a look of exhaustion. Her testimony was emotional and followed Bailey's narrative—the kidnapping, life in the closet, the tapes she made for her captors. She often appeared distraught or broke into tears. The session ended with Patty's description of Cinque entering the closet, sexually assaulting her, and leaving. The next day, defense lawyers reported that Patty's mail, at one time consisting of 80 percent "hate mail," was now "predominantly sympathetic."[81]

November 4, 1975, drawing of Patricia Hearst, defense counsel F. Lee Bailey, and Judge Oliver Carter, one of many made by courtroom artist Rosalie Ritz. Courtesy of Rosalie Ritz. Bancroft Library, University of California, Berkeley.

The following week, under Bailey's direct examination, Patty told the jurors what they most wanted to know: why, in the aftermath of Hibernia, she had not tried to escape.

BAILEY: *Did you consider the possibility of escaping if the opportunity arose?*

HEARST: *It just—it didn't seem realistic anymore.*

BAILEY: *What did you think might happen if you tried to escape?*

HEARST: *I thought that the FBI would kill me.*

BAILEY: *Did you consider the claim of the SLA that it would be a politically wise move for the FBI to kill you and then blame it on the SLA to make them unpopular?*

HEARST: *Yes.*

During questioning about the combat and weapons training she had received, she offered an explanation for the events at Mel's:

BAILEY: *What were you told to do?*

HEARST: *That if anybody ever got in trouble, that you were supposed to fire on the people that were attacking them and help them get away; and, that it was in the codes of war, too, that—that anyone who didn't do that would be killed. . . .*

BAILEY: *What was the penalty for failure to rescue a comrade in trouble as it had been described to you?*

HEARST: *Death.*

And she made an effort, perhaps less than fully persuasive, to account for her behavior after her arrest—the raised fist, the "urban guerrilla" response:

HEARST: *At first I told her I didn't have a job.*

BAILEY: *Then what did she say?*

HEARST: *She said, "We need an occupation."*

BAILEY: *And what was your response?*

HEARST: *I just shook my head and said I didn't have a job.*

BAILEY: *All right. And then what did she say?*

HEARST: *She said, "We have to have an occupation," and so I said, "Urban guerrilla." . . .*

BAILEY: *At some point when you were coming down to the court, or leaving it . . . did you place your hand up in this fashion (indicating)?*

HEARST: *Yes.*

BAILEY: *Why did you do that?*

HEARST: *Because I mean I knew that's what I was supposed to do.*[82]

Browning's cross-examination began late in the afternoon on February 18, and his first questions were unexpected. The Patty Hearst he offered to the jury was not brainwashed or terrified, but rather a naïve, sheltered young woman in the throes of discovery, developing a social conscience:

BROWNING: *And was it not quite shocking to you to live as you did after the kidnapping in the poverty areas of San Francisco? . . .*

HEARST: *Yes.*

BROWNING: *And you developed an awareness of many problems, did you not, that you had never thought of prior to your kidnapping?*

HEARST: *Right, that's true.*

BROWNING: *And would it be fair to say that what you saw and heard and talked about made quite an impression on you?*

HEARST: *Yes.*

BROWNING: *And did you, as a matter of fact, conclude that changes in the society would have to be made, that they were needed, changes that you had theretofore perhaps not realized should be made or needed?*

HEARST: *In a sense, yes.*[83]

Under Browning's questioning, Patty revealed that after the kidnapping she had read many books with a political or social message, including George Jackson's *Blood in My Eye*, Toni Morrison's *The Bluest Eye*, Rita Mae Brown's *Rubyfruit Jungle*, which she said had "impressed" her, and another she referred to as *Labor Story* (perhaps Aleine Austin's *The Labor Story*). Further questions elicited a list of the books that had been found in Patty's bedroom when she was arrested: Patrick Renshaw's *The Wobblies*, G. William Domhoff's *Who Rules America*?, and Richard Gott's *Guerrilla Movements in Latin America*.

BROWNING: *So, in essence, you were—would it be a fair statement to say—quite interested in revolution, social change? . . .*

HEARST: *I would say I was interested in social changes.*[84]

With Patty's help, Browning had suggested that Patty had been changed by contact with the SLA, and that the change had come through books and ideas, rather than violence and fear. Then, again with Patty's help, he confronted the "brainwashing" defense, as yet undeveloped but waiting in the wings. The context for his attack was the sixth tape, on which Patty had denied being brainwashed and had called the idea "ridiculous to the point of being beyond belief."

BROWNING: *Do you recall those words?*

HEARST: *Yes*

BROWNING: *And Angela Atwood supplied you with those words, is that right?*

HEARST: *Yes*

BROWNING: *At no time did you believe that you had been brainwashed?*

HEARST: *No. . . .*

BROWNING: *Do you now feel that you had in fact been brainwashed at any time, Miss Hearst?*

HEARST: *I'm not sure what happened to me.*[85]

Browning pressed his advantage, using Patty's own words to define, and tame, the word "brainwashing." The words were drawn from the "Tania Interview," the document drafted by Patty and the Harrises during the missing year, long after and far away from the horrors of the closets:

> I feel that the term "brainwashing" has meaning only when one is referring to the process which begins in the school system and is continued via the controlled media, the process whereby the people are conditioned to passively take their place in society as slaves of the ruling class. Like someone said in a letter to the *Berkeley Barb*, I've been brainwashed for 20 years, but it only took the SLA six weeks to straighten me out.

Here was Patty the radical, spouting leftist educational and media theory of the sort that Colin Greer, Joel Spring, Herbert Schiller, and Ivan Illich were then publishing, defiantly asserting that she had been educated by the SLA, not brainwashed.[86] Of course, she could have been brainwashed—brainwashed by another definition—when she made that claim. But if it were true—if Patty had been won over and educated by the SLA, if her worldview had in fact changed—then Patty had become at once more clearly guilty of having voluntarily assisted in the Hibernia robbery and more dangerous. If it were true, Patty now stood for all women who might reject wealth, patriarchy, domesticity, and naïvete to embrace an inclusive, worldly, savvy social feminism.[87]

Perhaps Browning understood that there was danger in emptying Patty out, in presenting her as a tabula rasa on which the SLA had been able to write its message. If, indeed, Patty had no core, no preexisting inner being, it followed that she had been and would be whatever others wanted her to be: a cipher, an object, a victim. And so he teased from this ordinary young woman just enough substance to make it credible that her transformation into a member of the SLA had come at least partly from within, from choices she had made that were at least superficially consistent with her character.

BROWNING: *Prior to your kidnapping, did you consider yourself a submissive person?*

HEARST: *Not really, no.*

BROWNING: *As a matter of fact, you generally stood up for what you believed in and said what you thought, didn't you?*

HEARST: *For the most part, yes.*

BROWNING: *Sure. And you, occasionally, had arguments with your parents; didn't you?*

HEARST: *We had discussions. We didn't have arguments. . . .*

BROWNING: *Did you have some run-ins occasionally with your teachers at school, various schools?*

HEARST: *Yes.*

BROWNING: *What about your employers? You worked at Capwell's for a period of time. . . . Isn't it a fact that you felt that the employees of Capwell's were being exploited?*

HEARST: *I felt like that there should be a union at the store. . . .*

BROWNING: *You were fairly vocal about that, weren't you?*

HEARST: *No, I wasn't.*[88]

The Patty Hearst Browning wanted the jury to see was a decision-making woman who had made choices: the choice to have a relationship with Willie Wolfe (Cujo) and the choice not to attempt escape. The former seemed doable; Patty, as Tania, had had some sort of ongoing, intimate relationship with Cujo, had worn the Olmec monkey he had given her, and had, on the seventh tape (recorded after the Los Angeles fire, and Cujo's death), referred to him as "the gentlest, most beautiful man I've ever known." But Patty proved an uncooperative witness on the matter. On the stand, she denied that she loved Cujo, insisted that he had raped her in the Daly City safe house, and set a neat trap for Browning when she confirmed that she "had a strong feeling about him." The prosecutor took the bait:

BROWNING: *Well, what was that feeling?*
HEARST: *I couldn't stand him.*[89]

To press the important issue of Patty's failure even to contemplate seriously an escape, Browning turned to her cross-country car trip with Jack Scott and his parents, which would seem to have afforded her ample opportunities to flee or contact the authorities. At that point, too, Patty, although still fearful, was no longer subject to the coercive reeducation methods she had arguably earlier experienced. Browning initiated several exchanges on the subject, including this one, from February 20:

BROWNING: *Well, didn't you tell us this morning that you could have telephoned in motel rooms when you were going across country with Jack Scott?*
HEARST: *It wasn't possible for me to call.*
BROWNING: *Why not?*
HEARST: *Because I couldn't do it.*
BROWNING: *You couldn't do it because you were afraid if you called they would kill you; right?*
HEARST: *Yes. And I was afraid of the FBI, too.*
BROWNING: . . . *Did it ever occur to you, Miss Hearst, to pick up a telephone in a motel room where nobody else was around and make an anonymous call and tell the police somewhere where the Harrises were so they would arrest the Harrises?*
HEARST: *Yes.*

BROWNING: *Why didn't you do it?*

HEARST: *Because I was afraid.*

BROWNING: *What were you afraid of?*

HEARST: *Because they aren't the only people running around that are like that.*

BROWNING: *Well, how many other people had you seen in association with the Harrises?*

HEARST: *I had heard of many other people. . . . And seen some people. . . . There were many other people that could have picked up where they left off and if they'd wanted me dead, all they had to do is say that that's what they want. . . .*

BROWNING: *Well, what caused you to believe that they could simply, by the snap of their fingers, if they were safe in police custody, if you turned them in, that they could . . . have you killed?*

HEARST: *It's happening like that now on the street.*

BROWNING: *It's happening now?*

HEARST: *Yes.*

BROWNING: *What do you mean, Miss Hearst? . . .*

HEARST: *Well, San Simeon [the Hearst country estate] was bombed, my parents received a letter threatening my life if I took the witness stand, their lives if I took the witness stand, and they [the New World Liberation Front] wanted a quarter of a million dollars put into the Bill and Emily Harris defense fund.*[90]

The "missing year"—especially the period from September 1974, when Patty arrived in Las Vegas, to September 18, 1975, when she was arrested with Wendy Yoshimura in Oakland—proved even more difficult for the defense. On February 23, three days after she had tried to explain her failure to telephone the police on her way to Pennsylvania, Patty took the Fifth Amendment forty-two times, refusing to incriminate herself by testifying about events during the portions of the missing year when she had been involved in additional criminal activity.

Was Patty lying? Were her fears legitimate? Was she paranoid? Did her taking the Fifth Amendment when asked about later activities reveal anything about the Hibernia robbery? The jury would decide, and its decision would of necessity be based almost entirely on what was known of Patty's conduct and on perceptions of her truthfulness. Those with other concrete information were few, and most of them had died in the Los Angeles fire. But the trial did bring out one witness who claimed to have knowledge of the SLA's *intent* with regard to Patty, and that knowledge could be used to assess the legitimacy and level of Patty's fear, and perhaps to shed light on her state of mind inside the Hibernia Bank. Ulysses Hall had known Donald DeFreeze in the early 1970s, when both men were inmates at Vacaville State Prison. In April 1974, after hearing about the Hibernia Bank robbery, and curious as to why DeFreeze would "take a person . . . that's worth millions of dollars and use her [i.e., endanger her] in a $10,000 robbery," Hall made contact with DeFreeze, and they talked on the phone. As Hall recalled the conversation, DeFreeze told him that he had "three alternatives."

BAILEY: *What were they?*

HALL: *One was to kill her——*

BAILEY: *Uh-huh.*

HALL: *You know, but I—like I'd been knowing him a long time and he really wasn't a killer, you know. . . .*

BAILEY: *But he said that was one of the alternatives?*

HALL: *One.*

BAILEY: *What were the other two?*

HALL: *The other one was to send her home. . . . But just to cut her loose would be to front off [damage] the SLA. . . .*

BAILEY: *You mean if she was sent home, they might get busted?*

HALL: *Yes. . . .*

BAILEY: *What was the third alternative?*

HALL: *Number three was to put her in a position where she would become a part of them or a part of the group or, should I say, use the word "front her off" again; front her off where actually the FBI, the CIA, whatever, would be looking for her as well as them. . . .*

BAILEY: *You mean make her a fugitive?*

HALL: *Yes, right. . . . And the only people that she could actually look for—I mean look for help to would be them and I say the trick didn't work because she's here today on trial.*

BAILEY: . . . *You said he didn't trust her.*

HALL: *Yes, he said he didn't trust her. . . . So he said that he had to make her prove herself. . . . And he told her that if—I mean that at the robbery, that he was going to have a gun pointed at her head.*

Browning's cross-examination marked Hall as a user of narcotics. But the defense had scored a point. As the courtroom emptied, Catherine Hearst embraced F. Lee Bailey.[91]

In mid-March, as the trial was winding down, an exasperated F. Lee Bailey would say in open court (though not in the presence of the jury), "I would not have introduced any psychiatric evidence if I didn't have to explain Mel's." For Bailey, "Mel's" was the quintessential "after conduct" event. "After conduct" events (i.e., those after Hibernia) weakened efforts by the defense to ascribe Patty's conduct to "duress," a defense firmly entrenched in the law but subject to strict standards. Patty's conduct at Mel's and her acquiescence during the missing year tended to undermine the claim. Duress, according to Browning, required "well-founded fear of impending death or serious bodily injury," and Judge Carter would offer something very close to that definition in his instructions to the jury, adding that the compulsion associated with coercion or duress "must be present, and immediate." Carter had early on demonstrated skepticism with regard to the duress defense, at least as it applied to the Hearst case. In September 1975, responding during a bail hearing to the arguments of Terence Hallinan (then Patty's lawyer) that Patty's status as a kidnap victim colored her activities as a fugitive, Carter appeared uncompromising. "That is a kind of mental diversion," he said. "I'm not going to deal in improbabilities and intangibles of that kind." What was crucial, he added, was that Hearst and the SLA had "announced to the world their revolution against our system . . . they've said it in loud and clear terms, and punctuated it with gunfire."[92]

The judge would prove no more sympathetic to a defense based on something like brainwashing, and this defense, unlike duress, had no status under the law; acquittal on that basis would have been unprecedented.[93] However, the brainwashing argument had at least two advantages. On the one hand, it offered receptive jurors a way to understand Patty's activities in the "after conduct" phase, when the threats necessary for the duress defense might seem to have been less "present, and immediate"; on the other hand, it allowed Bailey, and several witnesses, to present Patty Hearst analogically, in a series of images, each of which would presumably evoke sympathy: Patty as Korean War POW, Patty as Vietnam veteran, Patty as concentration camp survivor, Patty as Communist victim, Patty as zombie.

The first of the defense's brainwashing experts was Dr. Louis Jolyon West, who took the stand on February 23, a Monday, and testified for more than two days. Dr. West was professor of psychiatry and chair of the Department of Psychiatry at UCLA. As one of four court-appointed professionals, he had interviewed Patty for more than forty hours after her arrest. Based on the results of research on repatriated veterans, which he had conducted in the 1950s, West likened Patty's experience to that of American pilots captured during the Korean War who had made propaganda broadcasts for the Chinese Communists or given information to the enemy. Rejecting the vernacular term "brainwashing," West argued that the American pilots, and Patty too, had been subject to "coercive persuasion." For West, that term encompassed the sort of "forceful interrogation" that Cinque had used on Patty, as well as the use of isolation, darkness, and control of bodily functions to generate the combination of "debility, dependency and dread"—"DDD," he sometimes called it—that West and his research colleagues found had produced "compliant behavior" in over 60 percent of the pilots studied (by contrast, only 5 percent had mustered the level of resistance that the study labeled "heroic"). West also cited a post–Korean War Air Force training program, designed to help pilots resist these techniques, in which after three days of simulated coercive persuasion a number of pilots had developed "an uncommon terrible fear that they felt out of all proportion to what the reality of their situation was." Under the verbal and physical assault of the SLA, West argued, Patty had similarly succumbed, had become "numb with terror" and, like the Korean War pilots, convinced that what was happening to her was her fault. "It was a pretty classical example actually of what we could call coercive persuasion. She was persuaded to take on a certain role and she complied with everything they told her to do. . . . For her, it was to be accepted [by the SLA] or be killed." For West, the Korean War pilots and Patty deserved to be understood as victims of impossibly difficult situations, in which escape was unthinkable.[94] To blame the pilots or to blame Patty for not trying to escape—to blame the victim—would be inappropriate and wrong.

According to West, Patty was in the "role" of compliant victim when the "unexpected crisis" took place at Mel's, and she reacted by doing what she had been taught to do. Her first words to the Harrises as they sped away in the van—"Did I do right?"—reflected a childlike effort to perform her role as an obedient "private" for the "generals" she had been trained to follow and serve. Her clenched fist salute and self-description of "urban guerrilla" following her arrest were for West "the characteristic hanging on for a few days until you really know that you aren't still in enemy hands." In addition, based on his psychiatric examination, West testified that Patty's anxieties and fears had produced a reaction with "dissociative features"—lapses of memory, dreamlike states, a sense of unreality, the restriction of thought and feelings, even Patty's "downcast" eyes and facial "pallor" as he examined her—a state he compared to the "survivor syndrome" experienced by some victims of the Nazi concentration camps, who had stepped over the bodies of dead Jews but later could not remember having seen them. Recalling Patty's last words to him in a final interview, *after* the trial had begun, West emphasized Patty's deep commitment to survival: "My biggest worry right now," she had said, "is staying alive."[95]

Finally, West suggested parallels between Patty's experience and another famous case in the annals of brainwashing, that of Jozsef Cardinal Mindszenty, a Hungarian Catholic prelate who in 1948 was arrested by the Communists and taken to the prison at No. 60 Andrássy Street in Budapest, where he was stripped naked by police in front of a small group of bemused onlookers, given an "Oriental clown's outfit," and escorted to a cell. For thirty-nine days Mindszenty was beaten, drugged, deprived of sleep, relentlessly interrogated, and "broken" until, one day, he succumbed, signing a "confession" that was published in January 1949 as the *Yellow Book*, shortly before a three-day show trial. He was found guilty—of espionage against the Hungarian state and of leading an organization intended to overthrow the government—and sentenced to life imprisonment. Memories of the cardinal's experience had been rekindled with the publication of his *Memoirs* in 1974, and West's testimony reconstituted them for the Hearst jury. West argued that Mindszenty's description of his treatment was a "classical passage in the literature on coercive persuasion," adding that the "haunted look" on the cardinal's face in films of his trial, seen also on the faces of other victims of mock trials, was now referred to in his circles as the "Mindszenty look." West claimed to have found something like that look on the face of Patty Hearst—perhaps the "zombielike" appearance that troubled Alexander.[96]

During a cross-examination that took the better part of two days, Bancroft focused on undermining several aspects of West's testimony—the relevance of psychiatry in explaining Patty's conduct, West's authority and objectivity, the accuracy of the analogy between Patty's situation and that of the Korean War pilots—and on developing for the jury an explanation of how Patty could have taken up violent, criminal behavior without being brainwashed. Cardinal Mindszenty was not mentioned. Bancroft's first question set the tone.

BANCROFT: *Dr. West, do you recall who it was who said that "Perhaps the most insidious domestic threat posed by 'brainwashing' is the tendency of Americans to believe in its power"?*
WEST: *It sounds like something I might have said myself.*

And he had said it, in 1963. Over the next several hours, Bancroft pressed that initial advantage. Through rigorous questioning, he presented psychiatry as a soft science (even, perhaps, not a science at all), emphasizing that "reasonable psychiatrists may differ" in their diagnoses and interpretations—might differ, for example, in how they interpreted Patty's "urban guerrilla" remark. He revealed that West had broached the coercive persuasion idea to the Hearst family in June 1974, suggesting that West's apparent commitment to the brainwashing explanation might have biased his October 1975 examination and skewed his analysis of Patty's conduct. Using West's own research, Bancroft pointed out that none of the Air Force subjects West had studied had actually "defected to the enemy cause" (as Patty had, by implication, defected to the SLA cause); that some pilots (unlike Patty) had tried to escape, albeit without success; and that the Korean War prisoners had been subject to a much greater degree of isolation and sleep deprivation (Patty could hear the radio playing while in the closet and told West, "I don't think they woke me up in the middle of the night or anything like that. Once they did").[97]

On these and other issues, Bancroft foregrounded what he suggested was West's tendency to use his authority as a psychiatrist to *reinterpret* Patty's remarks to mean what he thought they should mean. This line of argument came to a head when Bancroft probed West for comments on the Trish Tobin tape:

BANCROFT: *And you heard there, did you not, the defendant describe that she was going to issue a statement if and when released on bail but that it would be from a revolutionary feminist perspective . . . ?*

WEST: *That was on the tape, sure. I also knew that Emily Harris was sitting about eight feet away from her when she said that. . . .*

BANCROFT: *Would your opinion be any different, Doctor, if the jail records show that Emily Harris wasn't in that room at all?*

WEST: *I'd find that quite fascinating; and, it would suggest to me that . . . to her, Emily Harris was a constant presence as long as she was there. If she felt that she was there and she wasn't really, I'd find that quite interesting indeed.*

BANCROFT: *In other words, whenever the defendant tells you something that turns out [not] to be true, you attribute it to some psychological cause?*

BAILEY: *I object.*[98]

Prosecutor Bancroft also sought to give Patty and her defense a leftist, "sixties" patina. With West's consent, he brought up the subjects and problems that the psychiatrist had studied in depth: drugs, hypnosis, hippies, alcoholism, homosexuality, civil defense, and racial violence. And Patty was presented not as the "naïve schoolgirl" noted in West's report, but as a rebel who had earned demerits at the Convent of the Sacred Heart, a boarding school, for "telling a nun to go to Hell"; who, according to her boyfriend, Steven Weed, had an "unparalleled" "capacity for sarcasm"; who had been described by a number of people as "independent"; and who had, before the kidnapping, used both marijuana and LSD.[99] This line of argument culminated in an exchange between Bancroft and West over the meaning of Patty's investment in individualism. West had written in his report that Patty had become embarrassed by the "implication of being a Hearst," and he argued that Patty's individualism was of an apolitical sort; that is, she simply wanted to be treated as a unique person rather than as a celebrity. Bancroft wanted the jury to draw a direct line from Patty's pre-kidnapping individualism to the much more political expressions of individualism on the tapes and in the "Tania Interview." West bristled at the suggestion and fought back. He called the tapes and the "Tania Interview" "unmitigated propaganda," comparable to the "propaganda broadcasts that were made by the American Prisoners of War and the statements they signed," and he denounced Bancroft's notion of individualism:

> What she was experiencing was the normal desire of a young person, 19 years old, to be differentiated and become an individual and her own person. And what's in [the "Tania Interview"] is the crassest perversion of the idea of individuality, where a small group of individuals goes around and kills other individuals in order to achieve their political goals. That is not individualism. That is terrorism. And there is nothing in her background to prepare her for that.[100]

The next witness, Dr. Martin Orne, was both a psychiatrist and a psychologist, and his testimony covered some of the same ground as that of Dr. West. Orne confirmed West's diagnosis of "traumatic neurosis" with a strong element of dissociation (i.e., intense role-playing, to the point where one becomes the role). But it also moved the case forward in three respects. First, Orne took up directly the question of whether Patty had been "simulating"—that is, lying in some fashion—since her capture. Based on his reading of the psychological tests Patty had taken, Orne testified that she had, indeed, been telling the truth. "It is just about impossible," he added, "to fool a truly experienced psychologist provided appropriate tests are given." Second, Orne shifted the comparison from the Korean War to the Vietnam War. In the early 1970s, Orne had served as a consultant to the National League of POW/MIA Families, focusing on the capacity of prisoners of war to resist interrogation. Prompted by Bailey, he linked Patty and the Vietnam POWs:

> I have seen some evidence of dissociation in a number of returnees from the Vietnam War. The Vietnamese were much more brutal really and much more extreme in their treatment than the Koreans [and their Chinese allies]. But I don't believe I have seen one quite as extreme as a dissociative reaction [*sic*] as Miss Hearst's.[101]

Orne was satisfied that Patty's dissociative reaction explained her behavior at the Hibernia Bank, the crime for which she was on trial. On cross-examination, he explained:

> I mean as far as I was concerned, the bank really wasn't the issue. The sporting goods thing is what I have to understand.[102]

The third contribution of the Orne testimony also came during cross-examination, in an exchange that found Bancroft floating a new argument to explain Patty's post-kidnapping conduct. Rather than ground Patty's actions in her own rebellious individualism or inchoate political inclinations, Bancroft here explored Patty as a tabula rasa, an empty vessel, open to new emotions and ideas:

BANCROFT: *Let me ask you, Doctor; people sometimes become acquainted and involved in political things where they previously have not been; isn't that possible?*

ORNE: *Of course.*

BANCROFT: *And people who—you've heard the expression "I got religion"?*

ORNE: *Yes.*

BANCROFT: *All right. Some people sometimes become, get religiously converted who were not previously religious?*

ORNE: *Yes, sir.*

BANCROFT: *So it's not always the case, then, that looking at a prehistory of noninvolvement in something is any good indicator of whether or not one would become subsequently involved in something?*

ORNE: *That's correct.*[103]

The last of the defense's psychiatric witnesses was also the most famous. Robert Jay Lifton, who took the stand on February 26, was professor of psychiatry at Yale University, a public scholar and the author of twelve books, including a seminal work on coercive persuasion—*Thought Reform and the Psychology of Totalism: A Study of "Brainwashing" in China* (1961)—and two, including *Death in Life: Survivors of Hiroshima* (1968), on the idea that would be the focus of his testimony: the survivor syndrome. For those jurors who could follow, Lifton described the *process* of coercive persuasion, which he had previously documented in the cases of prisoners of war: control of all communication (in Patty's case, the closet; "they seemed to know everything about me," she had told Lifton); assault on identity (criticism of her values, and those of her family); the experience of guilt (for being the daughter of a ruling-class family): fear-induced confession (the audiotapes); a sense of having betrayed one's loyalties (in calling her parents the "pig Hearsts" and helping to rob the bank); extreme death anxiety; symbolic death, the annihilation of the self; the offer of leniency (join the SLA and live); and adaptation, the quest for survival through "total compliance" though without ideological conversion. For Patty, this last step meant accepting Cinque's offer of membership. In the postrelease phase, victims of coercive persuasion, or of "massive trauma" events—the bombing of Hiroshima, the Nazi death camps, the lethal 1972 flood in Buffalo Creek, West Virginia—experienced symptoms of survival syndrome: a short-term tendency to stay within the adapted role (which would explain Patty's clenched fist and "urban guerrilla" remark); intense confusion about what had happened; and the persistent numbing of emotions and low affect (the zombielike demeanor Alexander observed, or West's "Mindszenty look").[104]

Sensing that Lifton's psychological and historical modeling of victimization might fall short of excusing Patty's failure to resist, Bailey asked his witness to comment on how American prisoners of the Chinese had handled their own, similar failures:

BAILEY: *Did you find in the recovery cycle of any of the prisoners, the Chinese prisoners, the question arising "Should I have done more? Should I have been more heroic in resisting?"*

LIFTON: *The question arose in just about every single western repatriate I interviewed in Hong Kong. They felt, for instance, it was enormously embarrassing, a source of enormous shame and guilt for—I am thinking of a particular Priest, a man in his early fifties . . . as he said to me again and again, "Somehow I should have been stronger." And the implication when they say this is, "I should have done this no matter what, even if they killed me. I should have stood up." But people don't function that way psychologically. We try above all to stay alive.*[105]

On cross-examination, Bancroft offered two challenges to Lifton's explanations of Patty's actions. The military analogy was flawed, he argued, because Patty had done something the prisoners of war had not:

> Now, Doctor, do you know whether or not any of the people involved in the thought reform process, or in the prisoner of war process, ever went and committed an overt act of violence against their own kind?

Then, having walked Lifton through the bank robbery, the incident at Mel's, and the "missing year," Bancroft appealed to the jury to see the psychiatrist's testimony as needlessly, and harmfully, complex:

BANCROFT: *Doctor, as a psychiatrist are you familiar with the term Occam's Razor?*

LIFTON: *I have heard something about it.*

BANCROFT: *Isn't that a principle that says the simplest explanation for most facts is the one most likely to be true?*[106]

Dr. Joel Fort, one of only two "expert" witnesses called by the government, would be on the stand for most of five days. His head was shaved, and he wore a mustache. His testimony began with the jury out and, curiously, with Assistant U.S. Attorney Edward P. Davis Jr. reading a statement Fort had made a month earlier that denounced sensationalized celebrity trials like Patty Hearst's, raised questions about the role of psychiatrists in criminal proceedings, and insisted that his own background—as a medical doctor specializing in "social and health problems"—made him as well qualified to give expert testimony as any psychiatrist (later he would claim that he had read 274 books and more than 150 articles in preparation for the Hearst trial). Psychiatrists, he explained under redirect, with Browning asking the questions and the jury present, were wrong to think of criminal defendants as "patient[s]" requiring therapy, or to "put them in a dependent pathological or sick position"; wrong to apply vague, even meaningless, concepts like brainwashing, coercive persuasion, or Chinese thought reform to the actions of prisoners of war or to Patty Hearst; and wrong to compare what had happened to her with the experience of concentration camp inmates.[107]

Patty was no victim. Indeed, for Fort, victimhood was an alien concept, one at odds with his reading of the human condition. Taking the stand on Monday, March 8, dressed in a green suit and green shirt, Fort referred to *The Survivor: An Anatomy of Life in the Death Camps*, a recent book by Terrence Des Pres that extolled the resiliency of human beings, the "tremendous strength of people to be able to surmount such terrible experiences and to walk out of those things and go on and live an average, if not a completely fulfilled life." Patty should have walked away, found a way out. Instead, she had robbed the Hibernia Bank "as a voluntary member of the SLA."[108]

Fort offered his own explanation for Patty's participation, or perhaps several, with a common core that he called "attitude change." He emphasized "actions" rather than "statements" and, based on interviews he had conducted with Patty, depicted her as a woman yearning for action, "searching for something exciting and meaningful in life," deeply impressed that the members of the SLA were willing "to die for their beliefs." Based on reports by others, Fort concluded that Patty was "an extremely independent, strong-willed, rebellious, intelligent, well-educated but not particularly intellectually inclined [person]," who in the months before her kidnapping had been experiencing "growing dissatisfaction" in her relationship with Steven Weed and taking drugs "for excitement, for relief of boredom, to try out new experiences." (Randolph and Catherine Hearst, called as defense witnesses, would later confirm one aspect of Fort's description, describing Patty as "strong-willed.")[109]

Although Fort's broad reading makes it difficult to pin down what he believed to be the critical catalyst for Patty's "attitude change," multiple references to "religious conversion" and an extended comment on the thousands of conversions that had produced the Unification Church, the "so-called Jesus Freaks," the Zen Buddhists, and the Hare Krishna group—which Fort apparently regarded as examples of a lunatic fringe—more than hint at his perspective. If Patty's "conversion" was not explicitly religious, Fort saw it as similar to the commitments many others had made to "exotic" religious groups, or to "hippie" or "radical" lifestyles. Patty's migration was similar, he argued, to that of the other white, middle-class women who had joined the SLA. They—and by implication, Patty—shared racial guilt, a "degree of self-hatred," a "lack of self-esteem." All were "part of a broad social movement that has been taking place in the United States in the 1960's and 1970's." Within two weeks of her kidnapping, Fort testified, Patty was "moving in the direction of a conversion or a commitment." By March 1, 1974—four weeks into what Fort saw as her "adventure"—she had become "a voluntary member of the SLA." Contradicting West, who had characterized Patty as a private in an army of generals, Fort pronounced Patty a "queen" in the army, reveling in the "status and recognition" that came with her new, media-hyped role. The "queen" remark made the next day's headlines.[110]

Harry Kozol, the government's second and last expert witness, was a slow-talking older man who spoke with a high voice and a bit of a lisp, much to the amusement of Judge Carter, Catherine Hearst, and others in the courtroom. He described himself as a physician with subspecialties in neurology and psychiatry, and he revealed a special interest in the "social violence" of young people: "Why are these kids [marching] in the streets? Why are some of them wrecking the computers, as they did in Toronto and Montreal?" He also had had some "intimate [as opposed to academic] experience" with prisoners of war, and some with kidnap victims. He too had interviewed Patty Hearst.[111]

Browning used Kozol to present to the jury a reading of Patty's sexual encounters while with the SLA that differed from the one she had offered in her testimony. Kozol commented on and interpreted the final SLA tape, made public on June 7, about two weeks after the Los Angeles shootout that had killed, among others, Willie Wolfe. "She really provided an obituary," Kozol said, "and the eulogy for the fallen comrades. And she speaks of Mr. Willie Wolfe . . . so lovingly and so tenderly and so movingly, at least this is my feeling as I listened to it." Then, recalling his interview with Patty, Kozol added:

> [I said,] "I am asking you, is that how you felt about him at that time?" She again became very much upset, began to shake and quiver obviously suffering. And she answered, "I don't know why I got into this God damn thing, shit"; and then got up and left the room terribly upset. A few minutes later she came back with her counsel. And my examination was over, no more time with her that day.[112]

Again, based on his interview with Patty, Kozol recast her initial sexual contact with Cinque as an episode of anger rather than lust. Based on the evidence that Cinque had (in Patty's words) "grabbed my crotch" without putting his hand inside her clothes, and that Cinque had been angry at Patty for lifting her blindfold, Kozol concluded that the incident was not a sexual assault:

> I did not look at that by him as a sexual assault. It was an angry—it had a sexual connotation—but apparently venting his anger.[113]

More important, Kozol helped the prosecution ground Patty's actions in her own growing dissatisfaction with the people around her, especially her parents and Weed. He offered the most critical assessment to date of Patty's pre-kidnapping relationship with Weed:

> She felt trapped in this relationship. She was very unhappy. I was [*sic*] asked her to tell me about herself, I asked her if she ever cried much, she said she never cried at all, or very little, until she was involved with Weed, with increasing disillusionment and disenchantment with him and his character, she cried more than she had ever cried before, she was very depressed and unhappy.

The relationship was unequal. "She did the cooking, then she would do the washing of the dishes and the pots and pans. Once in a while he would rinse something for her, but that was it." The upshot of all this, Kozol implied, was Patty's later attraction, nurtured by her growing friendship with Wendy Yoshimura, to women's liberation. According to Kozol, Patty's deep commitment to "revolutionary feminism" was all that remained of her SLA-generated concerns about race, poverty, nutrition, and housing. "I asked her why. She answered, 'Because I am a woman.'" The other issues were important, she had added, but, as Kozol recalled her perspective, "none of them were more important than the liberation of women from sort of a general enslavement which permeated society."[114] Kozol had all but said that Patty was in the Hibernia Bank because Steven Weed wouldn't do the dishes.

That wasn't good enough, Browning knew, and he asked Kozol to fill in the blanks. Patty had been indulged as a child, he testified, given "a great deal of freedom in many respects." The job at Capwell's made her "angry at what she had seen about the abuse of working people," and especially members of minorities. And then there was Patty's "subtle hostility" toward her parents. It all added up. "The girl who got kidnapped," Kozol concluded, "was a bitter, angry, confused person."

BROWNING: *Angry at what?*

KOZOL: *Angry at authority, angry at power, angry at hypocrisy, angry at hypocrite Steven Weed, who talked one thing to her, such as social reform and liberalism, and as soon as it looked as though he was getting associated with this family, had become more reactionary than anything she had ever heard at home or anywhere else. And she really was revolted by this man's sense of values and joined in some expression of that. So this is the girl who was picked up, in a sense with no place to go.*[115]

Browning must have been pleased. But he probably did not know that his witness was about to deliver one of the trial's classic lines. He picked up where he had left off:

BROWNING: *And how do those relate to the conclusion that you made, Doctor? Can you articulate for the jury?*

KOZOL: *This girl was a rebel. Whatever developed in the subtle interplay of a million experiences in her life, or multiple millions, she had gotten into a state where she was ripe for the plucking. She was in a receptive frame of mind. I don't think she was in a clear frame of mind, but she was in a receptive frame of mind. She was ready for something, she was a rebel in search of a cause or a rebel ready for a cause.*[116]

Patty Hearst as James Dean! Or rather as Jim Stark, as portrayed by Dean: the delinquent product of a domineering mother and a weak, vacillating, helplessly indulgent, effeminate father, a man incapable of offering the kind of advice that would initiate his son into responsible manhood. The comment shifted the site of Patty's rebellion from the 1960s to the 1950s, perhaps not the right strategy. But it also intensified the prosecution's focus on Patty's family as the primal source of her conduct. Although the family was not obviously dysfunctional, it was not difficult for the public, or the jury, to imagine that the Hearst millions had made a normal family life impossible or, conversely, that Patty's rejection of family privilege was a sign of ingratitude, perhaps brought on by association with countercultural values.

In any event, the idea that Patty's ordeal might be linked to the "family" had considerable appeal for a nation troubled by a rapidly rising divorce rate, a declining rate of marriage, and the sense that the traditional family, under pressure from forces as diverse as unemployment, feminism, and television, was no longer the cohesive center it had been only a decade earlier. That message was brought into millions of homes every Thursday evening in the winter of 1973, as viewers tuned in to watch a real middle-class family—Pat and Bill Loud, their twenty-year-old son, Lance, and the rest of the Santa Barbara, California, clan—falling apart on national television. Indeed, Lance's transformation on the show, from surfer boy to drag queen, shares the terrain of the bizarre with Patty's migration from country-club waif to guerrilla bank robber.[117]

More important, the phrase "rebel in search of a cause" opened the way for the jury to understand Patty's actions as motivated only by the vaguest personal need. No specific cause was necessary—*any* cause would do. Despite Kozol's earlier allusion to Weed's domestic shortcomings, this new twist meant that Patty's rebellion—and that of thousands of other, equally misguided young people—could be explained away without acknowledging any political objective as socially grounded as the liberation of women, the alleviation of poverty, prisoners' rights, or the end of the war in Vietnam. "Something," Joel Fort had said, "was missing in her life."[118] *Rebel without a Cause*. A movie title would help send Patty Hearst to jail.

Bailey approached cross-examination determined to cast doubt on the emerging idea of Patty as inchoate rebel. Through a series of questions, he suggested that Kozol had reached conclusions about Patty's family without talking to her mother, her father, or her sisters. In another exchange, Kozol admitted that his analysis of Patty's character was based in part on the story—now revealed by Bailey to be apocryphal—that Patty "once told someone at school that her mother had cancer to get out of an exam." And Bailey got Kozol to reinterpret Patty's concern for the exploitation of her coworkers at Capwell's, asserting that her interest, far from being "an indication of rebelliousness," was "very, very commendable." Bailey's second tactic was to reintroduce the basic elements of Patty's fear—Cinque, the closet, the attorney general's statement that Patty was a common criminal— in the hope that Kozol's responses would cause him to appear cavalierly unconcerned about any of that. Under Bailey's questioning, Kozol claimed that Patty had, indeed, been "free to go just as Cinque said," and that because Patty had survived—because she had not been killed—that Cinque's word had proved credible. (The jurors must have wondered at the reasoning.) Bailey also read at length from Cardinal Mindszenty's *Memoirs*, less to elicit a reply from Kozol than to once more raise the issue of brainwashing and to link Patty's predicament to that of the respected Catholic churchman.[119]

At the core of Bailey's cross-examination of Kozol (and of the preceding witness, Joel Fort) was a rather mean-spirited—but arguably essential—attempt to impugn the witness's competence and integrity. He opened by suggesting that Kozol's newly "accelerated" speech revealed a man anxious to have his testimony behind him. He questioned the relevance of Kozol's field of specialization, maligned his unfamiliarity with prisoner-of-war scholarship and the literature of coercive persuasion, revealed his lack of experience with young kidnap victims, and pronounced him unprepared to question Patty Hearst, having failed to have read the reports of the court-appointed psychiatrists. Bailey also probed Kozol's harmful interpretations of the SLA tapes. Under questioning, Kozol had insisted that the recorded messages could not have been rehearsed, that they had come from Patty's "own heart" and from her "own mind." But he also admitted that his opinions were only "impressions," and that on matters of language and speech patterns he was "no better than any other person."[120]

For all Bailey's hard work, the most memorable exchange of the Kozol cross-examination could not have pleased him—although Bailey had made it possible. It began with a question that reflected a minor theme the defense had now and then offered to the jury: that Patty's trial had been anticipated and desired by her kidnappers, and that her conviction, as a sign that others were convinced of her conversion, would amount to a victory for the SLA and other radical groups.

BAILEY: *Doctor, she is sitting in this courtroom today exactly as they planned, you know that, don't you?*
KOZOL: *Exactly as she chose, Mr. Bailey.*
BAILEY: *You say she chose to do that?*
KOZOL: *She chose. She chose a life which resulted in her being in this courtroom today.*[121]

Bailey's cross-examination of Joel Fort had been just as aggressive and more hostile, as one might expect given Fort's importance in constructing a plausible interpretation of Patty's behavior. His questions had focused on a Fort-authorized February press release, in which Fort questioned the objectivity and criticized the dominance of psychiatric experts in trials like that of Patty Hearst (at the time, it was not clear whether Judge Carter would allow such testimony). The press release also erroneously stated that Fort was the author of a book, *Expert Witness*, which had not in fact been published and, Fort admitted, never would be. And it made the curious claim, seemingly belied by Fort's desire to have his views published in *Newsweek*, that Fort sought anonymity and eschewed celebrity. Bailey hammered away at these and other contradictions, at one point reminding Fort that his picture had appeared in a Sunday paper accompanying an article titled "Bald Is Beautiful."[122] Nastiness abounded. At one point, with the jury not present but Fort on the stand, Davis lodged an objection to Bailey's "nonverbal effort to communicate sneers and whatnot to the witness by looking at his watch, lifting his eyebrows, curling his nose and other things." At another, Fort countered Bailey's attempts to paint him as a publicity hound. "Unlike yourself," he said to Bailey, "I have not chosen to have personal interviews with the media."[123]

On the critical matter of coercive persuasion, Bailey seemed to vacillate. On the one hand, he appeared bent on revealing Fort's ignorance of the field or, at best, his lack of reputation in it. "He hasn't practiced any psychotherapy," Bailey told the court, out of the presence of the jury. "And I should think I should be allowed to cross-examine him with respect to whether he could recognize a traumatic neurosis if he fell over one." On the other hand, he wanted the jury to know that Fort, while testifying on behalf of Leslie Van Houten in the 1971 murder trial of Charles Manson and his followers, had said that Manson's personal intensity had allowed him "to brainwash or produce a new form of thinking, a new pattern of behavior for the girls living in that group with Mr. Manson."[124] If Van Houten—the twenty-year-old murderer of Rosemary LaBianca—had been brainwashed, was Fort not contradicting himself, Bailey implied, in asserting that Patty Hearst could not have been?

Only a few witnesses appeared after the expert testimony was concluded, but three of them—an FBI agent, a UCLA professor of anthropology, and a Los Angeles Police sergeant—may in fifteen minutes have had more of an impact on the trial's outcome than the train of psychiatrists and psychologists that preceded them. FBI agent Thomas Padden told the jury that a photograph of Patty Hearst, taken before the fatal fire at the SLA safe house, showed a small stone figurine on a band around her neck, and that the same object had been found in Patty's purse on the day of her arrest. Anthropologist Clement Meighan identified Patty's figurine and another as inexpensive copies of a Mexican charm called an "Olmec monkey." And Sergeant Raymond Callahan testified that on May 17, the day of the Los Angeles shootout and fire, he had found a similar stone figurine beneath the body of Willie Wolfe.[125]

Closing Arguments

Closing arguments take place on Thursday, March 18, 1976, with both sides using a new podium set up close to the jury box. Judge Carter has briefly told the jurors what to expect, and has informed everyone present that no one will be able to enter or leave the courtroom while the arguments are in progress, an unprecedented directive that makes the courtroom atmosphere all the more intense. Journalist Shana Alexander, who has seen the entire trial, notes that Patty Hearst, starkly pale as usual, has arrived wearing "navy blue with a white bow at the throat." Browning, who will go first, wears a wrinkled suit and, according to Alexander, appears ill.[126]

After weeks spent listening to testimony from psychiatrists and other experts, and trying to figure out whether Patty most resembles a prisoner of war, the survivor of a Nazi concentration camp, or a rebel in the process of becoming a radical feminist, the jurors may be surprised at the content of Browning's opening remarks—and, indeed, at most of what he says during his two-hour presentation. The bank robbery is front and center. After concisely framing the issue—the government must prove that the "acts have been done willfully"—Browning immediately begins to marshal evidence to demonstrate Patty's "apparent voluntary participation": her handwritten comments in the "Tania Interview," her voice on the April 24 tape, the motion picture that shows her "swinging the weapon" in a way that, according to Browning, suggests voluntariness. Browning refers frequently to testimony about Patty's conduct inside the bank in the ten seconds or so *before* the bank cameras were activated, dissecting her brief interactions in those seconds for whatever they might reveal about her "intent." Then he replays the film, already seen by the jury two or three times, although not for a month or more. "The more you see that film," Browning insists, "the more you see in the film." Browning sees "practically no hesitation" in Patty's actions, no sign that she was concerned about what DeFreeze was thinking or what he might do. He sees her "agility," apparently another indication of voluntary conduct. And he sees that "no one, absolutely nobody, was ever pointing a weapon at the defendant in that bank."[127]

Convincing? Maybe, maybe not. The underlying message—what the jurors will recall when the fine points slip away—is that Patty's intent in the Hibernia Bank can be gleaned from "facts," from documents, from details. The particular details matter less than the *idea* of details. No need for psychiatrists or academics. A lawyer, armed with the facts and facing jurors with "common sense," will do.[128]

Browning is impeccably organized. If the jurors could take notes, they would have the beginnings of a lovely outline. Under the topic of intent—the voluntariness of Patty's actions—he lays out three subtopics: "circumstantial" evidence, the psychiatric testimony, and the defendant's credibility as a witness. Almost all of the circumstantial evidence of intent comes from *after* the bank robbery—the evidence that Bailey had tried unsuccessfully to have excluded—and Mel's is the "most crucial." Browning reads Patty's testimony on Mel's and notes where all the bullet holes were found, concluding that Patty was aiming, not for the top of the building, as she had testified, but "directly at Mr. Shepard [a Mel's employee] and the others that she saw." Without saying so, Browning has accused Patty of attempted murder. To Patty's comment that the shooting was a "reflex action," Browning delivers a wry rejoinder: there were "three reflex actions." "Is it reasonable to conclude," Browning offers, "that the captors would entrust their safety to their hostage, if that is what she were? Well, you can say, I suppose, the defendant simply put on a good act. Well now, we are getting into an area which draws a very fine distinction, ladies and gentlemen. Where does a good act leave off and voluntary participation begin?"

Aside from Mel's, the best circumstantial evidence of Patty's voluntary participation is her "flight"—the sixteen months in which she traveled across the country and back, living on one coast and then the other, with opportunities aplenty to escape. For Browning, the missing year demonstrates "consciousness of guilt." "You might say," he observes, perhaps too cleverly, "she didn't call us, we called her."[129]

Moving on to the psychiatric testimony, Browning seeks to persuade the jurors to disregard *all* of the expert interpretations and, again, to focus on the facts. He virtually ignores even his own witnesses; of the days and days Fort and Kozol spent on the stand, all that remains is Kozol's line, "rebel in search of a cause," which Browning cannot resist. He does, however, take each of the defense experts to task, albeit briefly. West, he says, went beyond the court's mandate to examine Patty and gave her a "road map" for her defense; rather than *ask* the defendant what she thought, he *told* her how she should think about what had happened to her. Moreover, West's analogy between Patty and brainwashed POWs is flawed, because the SLA was no "army" and DeFreeze had no expertise in mind control. Orne's Vietnam POW analogy similarly fails. As for Lifton's presentation on the methods of coercive persuasion, Patty was not isolated, and she knew (and acknowledged) that people were concerned about her.[130]

Although reluctant to say much about brainwashing for fear that even a critical comment might lend it a credence it shouldn't have, Browning knows he must deal with the issue. "Apparently," he suggests dismissively, mind control "was injected in this case by the defense in the hope that if duress does not stick to the ceiling, maybe something else will." In an attempt to keep the mind control argument from bleeding into and reshaping the duress defense, Browning draws a clear line between the bank robbery (for which, he asserts, the defense has offered only a duress defense) and everything after the bank robbery (when mind control might, he implies, be more relevant to Patty's actions). But *even if* the jury were to deem brainwashing relevant to the bank robbery, he asserts, it would apply to Patty no more than it does to any of the other upper-middle-class white women who became SLA "urban guerrillas." "Were each and everyone of them," he asks, "brainwashed?"[131]

Browning proposes that the jury ignore the psychiatric testimony altogether. Patty's duress/coercion defense, he insists, can be evaluated "on the facts." "You don't need a psychiatrist . . . to tell you whether [Patty was coerced to rob the bank]." Anyway, psychiatrists don't really have the skills we imagine them to have. "The psychiatrists," he declares, "weren't there at the bank robbery, they weren't there at Mel's, they don't have any ability to unscrew the top of a person's head and look in and take a picture of what the intent was any more than you or I do." Not surprisingly, he is especially critical of the defense experts—"professional and literary" people, "academicians," who talk about criminals as if they were "patients." But even if they were true experts—that is, forensic psychiatrists—there would be good reason to ignore their testimony. Experts have testified on both sides, Browning points out, and the result is a "wash transaction, one side washes out the other."[132] This is an outrageous argument—an assault, really, on the very idea of conflicting testimony, and on the criminal justice system itself. Are Browning and Bailey likewise a "wash transaction"?

Browning's last target is Patty Hearst or, more precisely, her credibility as a witness. Criminal defendants are not the most trustworthy bunch as a rule, he argues, and Patty has done and said many things that make her testimony suspect. The litany begins. Soon after her arrest, she signed an affidavit containing false statements. On the stand, she took the Fifth Amendment repeatedly, even when the court had ruled that it was not her privilege to do so. She claimed that remarks she made to Trish Tobin (she was "pissed off, Goddamn it," to be arrested) were influenced by the proximity of Emily Harris, who in fact was not in the room. Patty claimed she didn't know the weapon she carried into the bank was loaded, yet a witness had seen her drop ammunition clips that fit only her gun. The claim that throughout the missing year she had been too fearful to attempt escape is "too incredible to believe." Browning also stresses Patty's relationship to Willie Wolfe; the fact that she continued to carry the stone monkey he had given her proves that Patty was lying when she said, "I couldn't stand him." "She couldn't stand him," Browning says, "and yet there is the little stone face that can't say anything, but I submit to you, can tell us a lot."[133]

But Browning also has another argument, one that strikes at the core of the defense claim that Patty had been shocked into a deeply fearful state by the abuse in the closet. Browning reads from documents, some of them in Patty's handwriting, about the strong belief in radical feminism held by women in the SLA. "The men on the jury may wish to ask some of the women on the jury whether in their view a person strongly into radical lesbianism or women's liberation or radical feminism would ever permit herself to have been raped by one of the other males in that group."[134] Willie Wolfe did not rape Patty Hearst, he implies. The free will/choice argument is thus applied to sexual assault. Patty had chosen.

Another litany follows, this one seeking to ironize Patty's false statements, her incredible testimony:

> She asks us to believe that she didn't mean what she said on the tapes. She didn't mean what she wrote in the documents. She didn't mean it when she gave this power salute, this clenched-fist salute after her arrest. . . . She didn't mean it when she told the San Mateo County Deputy Sheriff that she was an urban guer-

> rilla. . . . She says the Tobin conversation wasn't the real Patty Hearst. The Mel's shooting incident was simply a reflex. . . . She was in such fear she couldn't escape in nineteen months while criss-crossing the country, or even get word to her parents or someone else. . . . It's too big a pill to swallow, ladies and gentlemen, it just does not wash. I ask whether you would accept this incredible story from anyone but Patty Hearst, and if you wouldn't, don't accept it from her either.[135]

It is Bailey's turn.

Bailey is as disorganized as Browning was organized, his presentation as disjointed and stumbling as Browning's was precise and lucid. "No one is ever going to be sure" what Patty was thinking, he tells the jury at one point. The confusion that permeates his closing might charitably be understood as his way of representing the doubt that the jury must have if Patty is to go free. Indeed, that is one of Bailey's themes: a "perplexed" jury (and the case will perplex even the next generation, he astutely predicts), a jury beset by "reasonable doubt," must resist the Perry Mason myth—that truth is knowable and will be revealed by the facts—and vote to acquit.[136]

Bailey is wary, too, that the jury will allow politics and social attitudes to affect its decision. He is concerned that jurors will convict Patty Hearst for what might be called populist reasons: because "she's a rich girl," because she's had a defense "better than poor people could get," even because they are trying to satisfy what they imagine to be the desires of those on the outside. He is concerned that the jurors will find fault with Patty for having valued "survival" over "freedom" (that is, for not having escaped), and he cautions them about the impropriety of letting that consideration influence their verdict. And he is concerned that jurors hostile to the liberal/radical zeitgeist of the 1960s and early 1970s might put Patty and her lawyer in that camp, accepting Kozol's argument that Patty was a "bitter and enraged child" who became a "rebel" (he avoids the phrase "rebel in search of a cause"), somehow linked to "crazy psychopaths" (no mention of the Manson "girls"). He offers a brief critique of each of these ideas, then seeks to identify himself with what he believes to be the jury's conservative sentiments. "I am not really a flaming liberal," he confides, adding that he "was one of the community that was offended by the fact that two anguished parents would give up all they would give up . . . in the one hope they could get their daughter back, and have her come on the air and insult them and call them pigs. The whole country was split up, we were all angry at her." Bailey admits to the jury that what Patty said and did assisted the SLA in its efforts to break down the social structure. But he also insists that Patty is not Squeaky Fromme or the Chicago Eight, the latter a reference to the political radicals tried in 1969 and 1970 for conspiring to incite a riot at the 1968 Democratic National Convention. The jurors, he says, would be wrong to inject their feelings about such political and social issues into their deliberations.[137]

Yet for all his efforts to keep politics *out* of the jury's deliberations, Bailey is not averse to employing a political framework when he thinks it would benefit his client. Aware of growing public anxiety about political kidnappings and acts of terrorism, Bailey once again suggests that the prevention of future acts of that sort depends on a verdict of not guilty. "The SLA predicted this trial," he argues. "They also predicted your verdict and persuaded her [that] coming back would get her twenty-five years. And if we can't break the chain at some point in their predictions, there are going to be other Patricia Hearsts."[138] The defeat of a radical political agenda requires Patty's freedom.

"Peripheral matters," Bailey asserts, must be put aside. These include the "awful" affidavit, which Bailey attributes to the flawed legal work of his predecessor; the audiotapes, which, Bailey reminds the jury, were introduced and played by the *defense*; and the events at Mel's, now reframed as having saved Patty's life ("If it were not for Mel's Sporting Goods, she would be dead, too, and you wouldn't have even a body to try").[139]

Bailey's closing is peppered with references to the expert testimony that has taken up weeks of the trial. He contests Browning's suggestion that the jurors are as able to judge Patty's intent as the experts, and he notes with disdain the government's effort to dismiss all expert testimony. "All they wanted to do was cancel out the three men whose expert help could give some meaningful advice in exercising your responsibility, and that is whether or not you have a reasonable doubt that Patricia Hearst was there with bells on, enjoying the experience of robbing a bank because she wanted to." Bailey calls Joel Fort "a psychopath and an habitual liar" and explains to a puzzled jury why he had treated him so roughly: "I thought that my duty was to cut his legs off so that he never disgraced an American courtroom again."

Although Bailey seems to know that his hope for acquittal may rest on the jurors' willingness to believe the explanations for Patty's conduct offered by West, Orne, and Lifton, he presents no systematic, clear summary of their testimony. The terms "brainwashing," "mind control," and "coercive persuasion" go unmentioned, the concepts reduced to a brief mention of the "new and better tricks" that in the end had overwhelmed even Cardinal Mindszenty. Without much enthusiasm, Bailey links Patty's taped statements to the confessions of prisoners of war, who believed that their words would be understood as delivered under coercion. He appears to have lost faith in a defense based on coercive persuasion.[140]

One idea does unify and bring a measure of coherence to Bailey's remarks, and Bailey must be hoping that it will carry the day. That idea is survival. "This is not a case about a bank robbery," Bailey defiantly announces in a direct challenge to Browning's presentation. "It is a case about dying or surviving—that is all Patricia Campbell Hearst thought about. And the question is, what is the right to live? How far can you go to survive?" To extremes, Bailey replies, citing *A Covenant with Death*, the story of a man who in 1923 killed his executioner, and noting the experience of sixteen Uruguayan teenagers who survived a 1973 plane crash in the Andes by eating the flesh of dead passengers. "We all have [a] covenant with death," Bailey lectures. "We're all doing to die and we know it. And we're all going to postpone that date as long as we can. And Patty Hearst did that. . . . And the manner in which she did it is the subject of this trial."[141]

Within this framework, Bailey offers the jury a narrative different from the bank-centered story Browning had provided. Bailey's narrative begins with Patty's brutal kidnapping. "In every kidnapping case," he argues, "there are only two kinds of victims, those that survive and those who don't." This narrative centers on the fifty-seven days Patty spent in a closet—"the closet, the closet, the closet, the closet, the one Dr. Fort thought was reasonably comfortable," an exasperated Bailey intones, pointedly asking the jurors if they thought *they* could "stand up to that closet." The story concludes with Patty in the bank. Recalling Hall's testimony about his conversations with Cinque, Bailey insists that Patty "was in the bank because they were going to kill her, they said, if she made a misstep." The "choice" Cinque offered—join or die—was no choice at all.[142]

In response to Browning's damaging story, based on the testimony of Zigurd Berzins, bank guard Eden Shea, and other witnesses who were inside the Hibernia Bank during the robbery, Bailey suggests that Patty's only goal was to avoid being killed. He tells the jurors that he had considered pointing a gun at them so they would know what it felt like to be in that position. "When you're looking at the business end of anything that fires a bullet, your attention is on that business end with one hope in mind, and that's that a bullet does not come out." Returning to the theme in his concluding words, Bailey insists that it has not been proved beyond a reasonable doubt that Patty wanted to be a bank robber. "What you know, and you know in your hearts to be true is beyond dispute. There was talk about her dying, and she wanted to survive."

Patty would later write that the case "had certainly been lost, or thrown away, during the closing arguments." For attorney Vincent Hallinan, who with his son Terence had briefly represented Patty before being replaced, Bailey had failed to offer the jury the only appropriate defense, one that acknowledged that Patty had in some degree been transformed into Tania. "If you're going to *give* a client a story to tell," he said after the trial, "for Christ's sake, give them one that can be believed."[143]

The Jury

The jury that was to decide the case was not to Bailey's liking. It had proved impossible to impanel jurors who were not familiar with at least some of the events in a case that had received such extraordinary media attention. That said, the jury was reasonably representative: seven women, five men; ten Caucasians, a Mexican American, a Japanese American (but no blacks). Its members were mostly middle class: a retired Air Force colonel (who served as foreman), a postal worker, an airline stewardess, a commercial artist, a housewife, a receptionist, a boat operator, a nurse, an airplane mechanic, a retired housing inspector, a dental assistant, a self-employed potter. Following the verdict, Bailey was pilloried by one critic for accepting a jury that included too many middle-aged women. "Any first-year law student," wrote Schuyler Davis to the *Los Angeles Times*, "could have told Bailey that a middle-aged woman is the worst possible choice to sit in judgment over a young, attractive, and well-to-do defendant."[144]

The jurors deliberated under instructions from Judge Carter that were, with one exception, unremarkable. The exception involved the relation between Patty's kidnapping and her participation in the bank robbery. Although Carter instructed the jury that a defense of coercion or duress could provide a "legal excuse" for Patty's role in the robbery, he also said that the compulsion must be "present, and immediate, and of such a nature as to induce a well-founded fear of impending death or serious bodily injury." The kidnapping was not enough. "That the defendant may have been kidnapped by others prior to the commission of the crimes charged is not alone sufficient to absolve her of responsibility for any subsequent criminal acts." Not long after Carter said these words, Catherine Hearst rose and left the courtroom, in tears. In an interview with the *Chicago Tribune*, she explained her reaction. "Judge Carter," she said, "seemed to totally overlook the fact that Patty was a kidnap victim. It was just too much for me to swallow. She would never have been in the bank if she had not been kidnapped."[145]

The Verdict

After deliberating for only twelve hours—obviously, there was more evidence than could have been taken up in so short a period—the jury returned with its verdict. Patty, who had been nervously crocheting in a holding cell in the federal courthouse, entered the courtroom, escorted by a female U.S. marshal. She stood, waiting. In a gesture of reassurance, Bailey patted her on the back. The sealed envelope made its way from the jury foreman to Judge Carter, who opened it, noted the verdict, and passed it to the court clerk. He arose and read: "We the jury, find Patricia Campbell Hearst, the defendant at the Bar, Guilty as to Count One of the indictment, Guilty as to Count Two of the indictment." Patty had been found guilty of armed bank robbery and the use of a firearm to commit a felony.[146] "Oh, my God," said Catherine Hearst, seated ten feet away from her daughter. Randolph Hearst muttered, "Oh Christ," rubbed his forehead, and stared ahead. Two of Patty's sisters wept. F. Lee Bailey went "white with shock," according to one account. Facing the jurors and looking away from her family, Patty, ashen-faced and impassive, turned to Bailey. "I never had a chance," she said.[147]

Sentenced to seven years in prison, Patty began serving her term on September 24, 1976. In January 1979, acting on the recommendation of the Department of Justice and perhaps responding to public opinion, President Jimmy Carter commuted her sentence to time served, justifying his action with the "but

United States District Court
For the Northern District of California

THE UNITED STATES OF AMERICA

vs.

PATRICIA CAMPBELL HEARST

No. CR-74-364 OJC

VERDICT

WE, THE JURY, find Patricia Campbell Hearst, the defendant at the bar, Guilty as to count one of the indictment

Guilty as to count two of the indictment

Foreman

FILED March 20, 1976, at 4 o'clock and 30 minutes P.M.

William L. Whittaker, Clerk

BY E.F. Driscoll, Deputy Clerk

The Patricia Hearst trial jury reported its verdict on this form, March 20, 1976. *Buffalo Courier Express* Collection, Buffalo State College, Archives and Special Collections.

for" argument: but for the kidnapping and her subsequent captivity, Patty would not have become a participant in the Hibernia robbery. The White House reported that in the month before the announcement, 97 percent of mail received had favored Patty's release, though mail received in the first days *after* her release was about two-thirds negative. Patty left prison on the first day of February, smiling and opening her jacket to show reporters a T-shirt with the words "Pardon Me" printed across the front. Around her neck was a medallion of green rhinestones, spelling out "SURVIVOR" and "2-4-74," the date of her kidnapping. In its first editorial comment on the case, Randolph Hearst's *San Francisco Examiner* called her conviction "appalling," "a miscarriage of justice." The *Portland Press Herald*, perhaps representing a new, more favorable view of Patty's case, titled its editorial "Freeing the Victim."[148]

Patricia Hearst leaves federal prison on February 1, 1979, having served twenty-two months of a seven-year sentence. She is accompanied by new fiancé Bernard Shaw and carrying her "clemency blanket," crocheted during her confinement. Courtesy *Sacramento Bee*/Michael Williamson.

Although the jurors had made a pact not to talk to the press, some did, and within forty-eight hours it was reasonably clear how and why the jury had voted to convict. From the beginning of the deliberative process, Patty's defenders were few, and not unyielding. During the first day's discussions, when no votes were taken, several jurors were relieved to learn that they were not alone in believing Patty guilty. "I thought I was the only one who didn't believe her," said one juror. "I thought I was the only one with doubts." Even so, the strain of moving toward conviction took its toll; some jurors cried, others vomited. Perhaps speaking for the majority, one juror described the trial's emotional trajectory: "When she was first on the witness stand, everyone's heart went out to her. How could you help it? We felt overwhelming sympathy for her, but then at some point in everybody's mind, the sympathy was outweighed by the evidence." Discussing the evidence, Norman Grim, the aircraft mechanic, emphasized Patty's failure to take advantage of opportunities to escape, as well as her performance at Mel's. "We couldn't really buy the reflex action explanation," he said of that episode. "She picked up one gun and emptied it and then picked up the other one. That kind of made you believe she was in the bank voluntarily." Also, he added, "She never contacted any of her family." Philip Crabbe, the letter carrier, said the Trish Tobin tape, on which Patty had expressed her anger at being arrested and her interest in revolutionary feminism, was "more important than some things" in arriving at the verdict.[149]

The six jurors interviewed by the *New York Times* agreed that the Tobin tape was one of several crucial pieces of evidence. Another was the monkey charm found in Patty's purse, which appeared to contradict her claim that she hated Willie Wolfe. "That was what changed my mind," said a woman juror. "I really saw how much she was lying. It just had to be lying, through and through." Also weighing on the jury were the eyewitness accounts of the bank robbery—perhaps especially that offered by Zigurd Berzins, a bank customer, whose testimony that Patty had entered the bank with spare ammunition conflicted with her claim that she did not know her gun was loaded—and the tapes Patty made while with the SLA, taken by the jury as revealing her true beliefs and feelings. The jury saw Patty's reliance on the Fifth Amendment to avoid testifying about her activities during the "missing year" as another sign that Patty was lying. "Eighteen months does seem too long," explained one juror. "Going back and forth across the country and everything—why didn't she escape?" The jurors who initially favored acquittal felt that Patty's lawyers had not given them much to work with except for the psychiatric testimony, which played only a minor role in the deliberations. According to one juror, Bailey "wasn't very helpful."[150]

Although none of these views seem clearly wrong or outrageous, neither do they suggest that the jurors took into account the complex testimony about Patty's state of mind. Writer Diane Johnson captured the jury's limitations in her 1982 book *Terrorists and Novelists*. "The problem for Hearst," she wrote, "was that the jury turned out to have no imagination. They could not imagine the kinds of life conditions people adapt to. They could not imagine that you might read the words of someone else into a tape recorder and not mean them, like poor Tokyo Rose, or could come to think you meant them. They could not imagine that they themselves, like most people, might clumsily assist, rather than resist, an assailant. They could not believe that there actually is such a thing as 'coercive persuasion,' or that revolution can seem attractive, or that the SLA were really assassins."[151]

Reactions

As measured by editorials, the views of columnists, and letters to the editor, public opinion of the verdict—unrestrained by the jury's need for unanimity and the appearance of objectivity—was more varied, and more attuned to the importance of the issues the trial posed for American public life. Money and class were front and center. Before the verdict, there was widespread concern that the daughter of wealthy parents, assisted by high-priced attorneys, would receive more than fair treatment, and that her acquittal would reveal a legal system biased toward those with means and influence. On that basis, at least, Patty's conviction was greeted with relief. "The jury's vision," claimed the *Richmond News Leader*, "snuffed out the potential for class antagonism that was present in the trial." A New York City public employee explained to the *Times* that "she had the best money can buy, but she got the right verdict." Showing restraint in its speculation, the *Detroit Free Press* stated no more than was obvious or possible: "Miss Hearst did not get off because she was rich. We do not believe she was *convicted* because she was rich." There were those who believed that the Hearsts' money had been poorly spent. The *Charleston Gazette* lamented the jury's hurried verdict and found Bailey's performance inadequate. Paraphrasing Adela Rogers St. John, a veteran reporter for Randolph Hearst's *San Francisco Examiner*, the *Gazette* remarked "that if Bailey is an example of a top-flight defense attorney, society is in real trouble."[152]

There was, conversely, a chance that Patty's wealth had made it *more* difficult for her to receive justice. Ronald Reagan, former governor of California and future president, found this view congenial. In a radio address taped in June 1978, Reagan argued that Patty had been a victim of class prejudice fed by media images of a "rich little girl," which had shaped the judgment of the jury and the American people. Imagining a scenario featuring "Patty 'Almost Poor,'" Reagan claimed that Patty's account of abuse and fear should have resulted in reasonable doubt. "Is Patty Hearst in prison," he asked, "because her family has money?"[153]

Reagan's view was more likely to be expressed on the op-ed page than in official editorials, and it seems to have become more common after Patty was sentenced and jailed. Writing for the *Chicago Daily News*, columnist Mike Royko captured the class hostility that lay just beneath the surface of the era and imagined how it might have affected public perceptions of Patty and her case. A few days after Patty's conviction, his column took the form of an interview with "Beergutt," who had decided that the guilty verdict was good for the country.

> "It will be a warning to the rest of them," he said.
>
> Rest of whom?
>
> "The spoiled rich kids. This will let them know that they can't get away with it."
>
> Away with what?
>
> "Robbing banks and having a good time and doing anything they want, while the rest of us have to work for a living and have a lousy time."
>
> Then you're convinced she's guilty?
>
> "Without a doubt. If she's not guilty, then why did she do it?"
>
> Do what?
>
> "Rob that bank. I could understand it if she was poor. But with all that money in her family, there's absolutely no excuse for robbing banks."

> But she was kidnaped.
>
> "That was her own fault. She wouldn't have been kidnaped if she hadn't been so rich. You don't see ordinary people getting kidnaped, do you?"[154]

Patty's defenders leaned hard on the basic idea that Patty was a victim. More than one newspaper resurrected the "but for" argument: but for the kidnapping, Patty would not have been in the Hibernia Bank. She was "a victim before she became an offender," wrote the *Cincinnati Post*. Had Patty not been "dragged screaming from her apartment" in 1974, asked the *Kansas City Star*, "would she have had any part in the crimes for which she was found guilty?"[155]

In their advocacy of Patty-as-victim, these commentators returned to the realm of psychology, virtually ignored by Bailey in his closing and, apparently, by the jury. Without mentioning brainwashing, the *Des Moines Register* drew parallels between Patty and "'Jesus freaks' and other converts," and hoped that the sentencing judge would appreciate that "the mind is a fragile thing." A similar mix of ideas was presented in a major *New York Times* op-ed piece, written by defense witness Robert Jay Lifton. Dismissing the term "brainwashing" as simplistic, while emphasizing "how fragile an instrument the mind can be," Lifton warned against presuming to determine Patty's state of mind during the bank robbery by reading backward from Mel's or from Patty's relationship with Willie Wolfe. What Patty was feeling inside the Hibernia Bank, he stressed, was the product of two months of physical and psychological abuse, including her victimizers' "clear message that they possessed, and would act upon, the right to determine who would live and who would die." Here was the point Bailey had hammered home in his closing: Patty wanted only to stay alive.[156]

This perspective was absent from most newspaper editorials. But in October, after Patty had begun serving her prison term, the *Los Angeles Times* published ten letters from readers, following up on a Phil Kerby column titled "Above All, Patty Was a Victim." All but one or two had been written by women, and nearly all asserted that Patty's conduct could be explained by her kidnapping, her incarceration in the closet, her need to survive, or brainwashing. "Patricia Hearst," Kerby had concluded, "was caught up in a series of actions that overwhelmed the mind and emotions of a young girl, who may have had little comprehension of what had happened to her." This analysis, occupying the space between coercive persuasion (or brainwashing) and temporary insanity, may have had no basis in the law, but it made sense to some people, and it made sense, too, of Patty's simple comment, made during the trial when asked if she had been brainwashed: "I'm not sure what happened to me."[157]

By and large, however, postconviction opinion celebrated the jury's verdict and reiterated the justifications offered by the interviewed jurors: the tell-tale monkey charm, the use of the Fifth Amendment, the Trish Tobin tape, and, most prominently, Patty's failure to take advantage of opportunities to escape.[158] Capping this predictable list was a curiously complex claim: that the jury had convicted Patty "on the basis of evidence," or "on the evidence," or "within the evidence." This claim seemed obvious enough on the surface, but it harbored important implications. One was that the monkey charm, for example, and Patty's invoking the Fifth Amendment constituted "evidence," while certain other things—Patty's testimony about her time in the closet, or West's about Korean War veterans—were mere opinion. The *Topeka Daily Capital*, whose motto was "In God We Trust," contrasted the government's "methodical presentation of evidence" with the "reams of opinion that [Patty] had been brainwashed or was under duress." These comments reflected a widespread, growing, and arguably populist disdain for "experts"—the psychiatrists and psychologists who had dominated the last weeks of the Hearst trial—now depicted as an overrated and corrupt bunch, practicing an "inexact art," feverishly bent on "rationaliz[ing]" Patty's criminal behavior, interfering with "the rest of us," as one editor put it, "who only go by practical judgment of right and wrong."[159] The belittling of expert opinion also allowed jurors and pundits to avoid coming to terms with the issue of whether there existed "reasonable doubt" as to Patty's guilt, a standard arguably met by the testimony of West, Orne, and Lifton.

Another assumption, made explicit by the *Arizona Republic* (its motto: "Where the Spirit of the Lord Is, There Is Liberty"), was that "evidence" stood against a different sort of information or argument, organized around the issue of causation, of "what may have led a defendant to a life of crime." The title of its editorial—"Patty's Clear Guilt"—reveals a desire to set aside the real problems of causation and responsibility that had been raised by the defense in the Hearst case. If, wrote the *Republic*, the jury had accepted Bailey's reasoning, then "any felon could claim that psychological conditioning in his home during childhood spawned criminal acts. A thief could claim that his family's pressure on him to acquire more belongings prompted stealing. The possibilities would be endless." The *Detroit Free Press* concurred, arguing that to excuse Patty's actions would have been akin to rationalizing criminal acts *because* they were committed by "the poor, or mistreated, or culturally deprived." At issue, claimed the *Baltimore Sun*, was "the concept of responsibility that forms the core of criminal law." The *Chicago Tribune* found the defense's "somebody made me do it" argument to be criminal-coddling kin to the 1966 Miranda decision that, it wrote, "has already been used to free a good many confessed criminals." And a student writing to the *Denver Post* maintained that if Patty had been acquitted, "it would show other countries that the United States is getting weaker while the underworld parties are getting stronger."[160]

Although these comments referred explicitly to the Hearst case, they were part of a more general conservative trend in ideas about crime, which had contributed to Patty's conviction. In the 1960s and early 1970s, criminal theory emphasized social and psychological causes—the criminal as victim—and justice theory emphasized rehabilitation and therapy. By the mid-1970s, as Americans experienced a new, troubling wave of criminal activity of all kinds, models of crime came increasingly to emphasize individual responsibility and free will, and models of criminal justice to favor punishment or simple retribution. Perpetrators were now understood to be evil or depraved, perhaps beyond help and rescue. These trends were apparent not only in the academic literature, or among politicians on the right, but also within the popular culture, where the "embodiment of evil," Charles Manson—a regular reference point for critics of the SLA and Patty Hearst—epitomized changing public perceptions of the criminal mentality.[161] Although Patty's jurors did not believe that Patty was evil or even depraved, they wanted to see her as responsible for her deeds, as acting from free choice.

The anxiety apparent in the attack on causation went beyond fears that the criminal justice system would collapse. Also at stake in Patty's trial were philosophical issues—"God-given free will" versus a "shallow determinism," individual responsibility versus the idea of the "victim"—that reflected fundamental concerns about the sources of human conduct and nature of human beings. In the *New York Times*, psychiatrist Walter Reich wrote that brainwashing, or what he labeled "internalized coercion," was the latest tear in the fragile legal fabric of free will, offering as it did a muddled, inferior "*kind* of will." Within this formulation, acts could be understood as a mixture of the voluntary and the implanted, and the person committing them *could not* be understood as having "an evil or vicious will." On the surface the impossibility of an "evil will" seemed positive and progressive, but it implied, of course, the corresponding absence of a "good will." In short, a brainwashed person could be neither "evil" nor "good."[162]

The implications of acts undertaken outside the framework of good and evil were explored by John Cogley, the former religion editor of the *New York Times,* in a brief essay widely reprinted in the days after the Hearst verdict. For Cogley, coercive persuasion through "mind-tampering techniques" was a fact of modern life, amply revealed in the Korean War and arguably the source of Patty's bizarre conduct. Indeed, Bailey had opened the trial by making just that argument: that Patty, as Cogley put it, was "clearly conscious; she was indubitably 'sane'—and yet she was not a responsible moral agent." Yet Cogley understood that Bailey had abandoned the brainwashing argument in his closing remarks, perhaps, Cogley reasoned, because he had sensed that the jury would be unwilling to deal with the "disturbing issues" it raised. To have persisted with a brainwashing defense, Cogley argued, would not merely have deprived Patty of free will, but would, as a consequence, have presented the jury with a brave new world indeed: a world without saints, without martyrs, without heroes.[163]

This interest in the shape of Patty's "will" helps explain the prosecution's development of Patty as a "rebel in search of a cause," as well as the attention that explanation received in the aftermath of the trial. On the whole, the government downplayed any possible "causes" for Patty's behavior, hoping to avoid the slippery slope that led from causes to "somebody made me do it" to "victim"—and to acquittal. Hence Browning's emphasis on "actions," especially Patty's actions inside the Hibernia Bank. Even then, however, it wasn't enough to catch Patty in an occasional discrepancy, picking up bullets when she had claimed not to know if her gun was loaded, or continuing to carry Cujo's Olmec monkey in her purse. If Patty's conduct—conduct that appeared to be both foreign to her nature and at odds with her zombielike demeanor in the courtroom—was to be understood as willful and chosen, Patty had to have a motive.

"Rebel in search of a cause"—Dr. Harry Kozol's fortuitous phrase—served the purpose, and several newspapers used it to explain or endorse the jury's verdict.[164] As a "rebel," Patty could be understood as motivated and willful, but only in a negative sense, her actions directed *against* something. The prosecution set up several plausible targets—her parents, Steven Weed's sexism, Catholic school discipline, the boring life of the wealthy—but as the second part of the phrase, "in search of a cause," conveniently suggests, none of these irritants really amounted to a "cause." There was no danger that the jury would acquit Patty because she had been victimized by the nuns at the Convent of the Sacred Heart, by Weed's refusal to do the dishes, or by too many elaborate birthday parties. By the same token, the phrase framed Patty's *resolution* of her situation as equally unimportant, trivializing her rebellion. Any "cause" would do, any port in a storm. To be sure, Patty had joined the SLA and robbed a bank, but her "search" might just as well have ended with, say, a stint in the Peace Corps or an affair with a married man. Patty had committed a crime and deserved to be punished, even though she was not really a bank robber and not really a criminal. She had been a "rebel in search of a cause"; the rebellion had been ordinary, but the search had gone haywire.

This view of Patty's rebellion as trivial and nonpolitical was consistent with Browning's closing and with the jury's narrow focus on the "evidence." But some newspaper editors, eager to indict the liberal and radical experiments of the 1960s as dangerous failures, preferred to see Patty as a political figure whose views and attitudes threatened the society. This take on Patty emphasized two issues. One was that Patty was a child of the 1960s, a product of Dr. Benjamin Spock's permissive child-rearing, a young woman "who needed to 'protest,'" a genuine "urban guerrilla" brandishing her "revolutionary rhetoric" against a benign and innocent "establishment."[165]

The other issue, also intended as a critique of the 1960s, involved what was understood as a basic flaw in Patty's character. According to the *Richmond News Leader*, Patty was—and had been, even before she was kidnapped—"a practitioner of situational ethics and personal gratification." "Short on moral capital"—that is, morally ungrounded—she was easily converted to the silly revolutionary ideology of her captors. Similarly, the *Winston-Salem Journal* described the "utter formlessness" and chameleonlike quality of Patty's character. A "moral drifter" lacking "ethical underpinnings" or a "set of sustaining principles," Patty could "move from victim to revolutionary and back to victim," always the opportunist, never troubled by "any sense of right and wrong." More disturbing, the *Journal* found Patty to be a representative figure, one of an "ever-growing number of Patricia-Hearst-like personalities in this country," each the product of a long, steady decline in "the transmission of ethics from generation to generation." The reclamation of social morality, then, required repudiating Patty's amoral situational ethics, and that meant putting her in prison.[166]

reading patty hearst

The Decline of Authority

We've reached the point in this essay where the author, judiciously sifting the facts and weighing the evidence, explains to his readers what was going on in Patty Hearst's mind at each stage of the story: in the closet after the kidnapping, while recording the tapes, when offered the chance to join the SLA, in the course of the Hibernia robbery, while firing off shots at Mel's, in the car headed to Pennsylvania, during the missing year. It's time to clear everything up, once and for all. Reveal the truth. The problem is, it can't be done. It can't be done for the same reason that the case attracted so much attention three decades ago: because there is no clarity to be had, no truth to be revealed—no truth of that sort, anyway. We can never know with certainty what Patty was thinking when she called her parents "pigs," accepted Cinque's offer, announced her presence in the bank, fired the second gun at Mel's, put the Olmec monkey in her purse, or failed, and failed again, to pick up a telephone and call the police.

As maddening as this indeterminacy may be, it is also revealing. One reason for the untidiness is the failure of psychiatry—the medical science of the mind—as an explanatory system. Compare that failure, and the assault on psychiatric authority during the Hearst trial, with the psychiatrist's role in Alfred Hitchcock's *Psycho* (1960), a late entry in an outpouring of psychiatry films in the post–World War II era. The film is justifiably famous for its taut narrative and shocking shower murder, but its final scenes are dominated by a police psychiatrist with a Freudian perspective, who at great length explains Norman Bates's misdeeds to those assembled at the precinct and, of course, to theatergoers, who have arrived at this point in the film not quite sure how to assemble what they have witnessed into a coherent narrative. The arrogant self-confidence of his presentation is typical of filmic portrayals of psychiatrists in the period, but it also owes something to the hubris of the moment—now identified with the presidency of John F. Kennedy—when for the American nation all things seemed possible, every problem could be solved, and everything could be explained.

By 1975 that confidence was gone, a victim of assassinations, Vietnam, urban riots, Watergate, the emergence of terrorism, and global economic forces that threatened the nation's dominance. Gone too, as Patty's trial revealed, was the sense that anyone, least of all a psychiatrist, could know what had happened within another person's mind. What remained was a surfeit of competing explanations, often couched in rhetorics of moral principle and politics, marking a fragmented, divided, and contentious society. *Psycho*'s authoritative and comforting psychiatrist/narrator had given way to multiple narrators or shrill advocates lacking the authority to carry the day, some of them just plain wrong. Modernism's exuberant confidence in progress, consensus, and science had yielded to postmodernism's doubts and multiplicities. Indeed, the cacophony of conflicting opinion on Patty Hearst recalls modernist architect Philip Johnson's historic venture into postmodernism, the AT&T building (designed in the 1970s, completed in 1984), its modernist shell and Chippendale top suggestive of postmodernism's enthusiasm for multiplicity, as if the building had been designed by two architects, narrated by two voices.

In that sense, the Hearst episode shares ground with Stanley Kubrick's *Barry Lyndon* (1975), whose protagonist is not knowable and whose narrator is not trustworthy, and with Terrence Malick's *Badlands* (1974), a story based loosely on the 1958 case of fugitive murderer Charles Starkweather (who fancied himself James Dean's "rebel without a cause") and his companion, Caril Fugate. Starring Martin Sheen as Kit and Sissy Spacek as his fifteen-year-old lover and companion Holly, the film eerily anticipates aspects of Patty's experience with the SLA. Although Holly is not kidnapped, she is, like Patty, drawn swiftly into a world of adventure, violence, and crime, and her reactions to that world remain as unfathomable as those of Patty Hearst. Holly's uninflected voice-over narration accompanies Kit's killing spree but fails to explain his motives or to describe adequately her feelings. When Kit murders her father (Warren Oates), all she can muster is "Maybe we oughta tell someone about this." Later, after Kit has shot and killed his friend Cato, Holly says, "I didn't feel shame or fear, but just kinda blah." Like Patty, she seems not to contemplate escape: "The world was like a faraway planet to which I could never return." When Kit finally seems trapped and yet can't give himself up, she refuses to go with him but cannot explain why: "I just don't want to go."[1]

Because Patty's motives and intentions were, from the beginning, unclear, her case allowed Americans—her parents, the lawyers, journalists, the jury, ordinary folks of all persuasions and from all walks of life—to project their values, ideals, and concerns onto the persona of Patty Hearst and to interpret her conduct as they saw fit. And so she became, for one person or another, or one group or another, a terrorist, a misguided sixties radical, a woman with a gun, a rich bitch, a victim of sexual abuse, a confused, frightened girl, a bored woman awakening to a life of risk and purpose, the veteran of a new and nasty kind of war, a brainwashed zombie, a survivor. A judicious sifting of the elements of the narrative reveals some of these labels to be more accurate than others, better grounded on available evidence, less self-interested, less political. But a surer way to give the case meaning is to think about how these disparate, incompatible ideas of Patty—these projections—were shaped by, and emerged from, American society and culture in the 1970s.

Many of the labels applied to Patty expressed concern and anxiety about the nature and content of political radicalism. This issue was undeniably important; Patty's kidnapping followed more than a decade of radical activity on the part of youth, women, minorities, and, of particular interest for the Hearst case, prison populations. For many Americans in 1974, recent history consisted of a chain of unsettling and threatening events: the 1964 Free Speech Movement in Berkeley; race riots in Watts, Harlem, Newark, Washington, D.C., and many other cities; violent confrontations between antiwar demonstrators and police at the 1968 Democratic National Convention in Chicago; the brutal murders, in 1969, of actress Sharon Tate and Leno and Rosemary LaBianca by Charles Manson and his "family"; the killing of students by National Guard troops at Kent State University in May 1970; the 1969 occupation of Alcatraz Island by Native Americans; the deadly 1971 uprising among inmates at New York's Attica Correctional Facility; actress Jane Fonda's controversial visit to Hanoi in 1972. Also in 1972, the killing of eleven members of the Israeli delegation to the Munich Olympics by Arab guerrillas raised public consciousness of a new threat, that of international terrorism.

By the mid-1970s, most Americans were caught up in a search for normalcy of an intensity not seen since the 1920s, a search that, in a sense, required Patty's conviction as a sign that the excesses of the 1960s and early 1970s had been repudiated, that a political corner had been turned, that terrorism would not be tolerated. The defense also recognized that desire; more than once, albeit ineffectually, Bailey had insisted that only an acquittal would prevent more political kidnappings and bring that form of terrorism to a halt.

Yet even convicted, Patty would represent a difficult social challenge. An ordinary young, white woman, born to wealth but living the humdrum life of the middle class, seemingly without preexisting political commitments, had somehow taken on radical political views and embarked on a life of crime. If this could happen to Patty, it could happen to anyone, and the government did not want to suggest that just *anyone* could so quickly be converted to an antisocial perspective or ideology, especially in the mid-1970s, when radical activity seemed finally to be in decline. How then, to convict Patty and repudiate her conduct without portraying her as "everywoman"? How to answer the question "What makes a radical?" without suggesting Patty's trajectory as a template for legions of the disaffected?

In negotiating these questions, the government employed a variety of strategies. One strategy, pursued by both the prosecutor and some in the press, was to suggest that Patty, the Harrises, and the SLA were anachronisms, pathetic remnants of an earlier era, caught up in a fantasy world of "search and destroy" missions and other thrill-seeking adventures adapted from a Vietnam War that was over and done with. And perhaps they were. Another strategy, represented in the phrase "rebel in search of a cause," was to cast Patty as an accidental radical, suggesting that her disaffection could have found an outlet in *any* cause. That Patty's quest had ended with the SLA was just bad luck. This approach, too, avoided the uncomfortable possibility that Patty's migration from moderate unhappiness to armed rebel might be a model for many other young women. A third strategy was to present Patty's attraction to radicalism not as a gradual and thoughtful development, but as a cultlike conversion, an emotionally overwhelming moment in which Patty "got religion."

The Fragile Self

The discussion about whether and how Patty had changed or been changed—had she been brainwashed, converted, coerced, persuaded? had she "seen the light"?—took place within the context of a larger, and no less intense, discussion about the nature of human beings, about the self. Was Patty's transformation evidence that modern people lacked a stable core, that the self could be dramatically reconfigured just like *that*? The problem was not new. In his celebrated autobiography, first published in 1791, Benjamin Franklin had reveled in the discovery that he could remake himself for a new life in Philadelphia by changing and controlling his outward appearance. In "The Man of the Crowd," a short story from 1840, Edgar Allan Poe revealed his discomfort with an urban society that had muted individuality and made strangers indecipherable and, frighteningly, unknowable.[2] Even so, a belief in the concept of "character"—that indestructible essence of an individual self—persisted into the twentieth century, when, historians agree, it was gradually replaced by a mutable self, known as "personality." "The social role demanded of all in the new culture of personality," wrote Warren Susman, "was that of a performer. Every American was to become a performing self."[3]

In the 1970s fans of rock music could observe something like that in the theatrical presentations of David Bowie, who with *The Rise and Fall of Ziggy Stardust and the Spiders from*

Mars (1972) and other albums offered a chameleonlike persona through which, writes critic Tom Carson, he "redefin[ed] stardom as a series of brilliant impersonations."[4] (One recalls the *Arizona Republic*'s insistence that Patty, flexing her malleable personality, had "acted out the role" of a hardened criminal.)[5] Bowie's equivalent in the visual arts was Cindy Sherman, a conceptual photographer (just a month older than Patty) who also trafficked in multiple identities. Sherman found her trade in the mid-1970s at Buffalo State College in upstate New York, where she learned to take pictures, and at Hallwalls, an avant-garde arts space in Buffalo, where she first exhibited. Moving to New York City in 1977, she produced the *Untitled Film Stills*, a series of self-conscious, voyeuristic photographs for which she herself posed, each presenting a cliché of female life in the 1950s: the sexy librarian, the beleaguered housewife, the wary career girl in the city. Although the viewer is tempted to imagine each of the women she depicts as a particular person with a particular story, that reading is contested by the evocation of publicity photos for B movies and the repeated appearance of Sherman, in performance. (Think of Patty, locked and loaded in the Hibernia Bank, a particular person with a particular story, but also costumed, constructing her identity as Tania.)[6]

Theorists of "identity" arrived at a similar conclusion, arguing that twentieth-century developments, including the proliferation of bureaucracy and the rise of consumerist and celebrity cultures had undermined the elements of the stable self and made identity—that is, "authentic individuality"—increasingly difficult to achieve.[7] In the late 1960s, psychologist Walter Mischel launched the "situation versus personality" debate, which remained vigorous throughout the 1970s. Using "personality" to mean the stable traits of an individual, Mischel argued that behavior was most often determined not by the inherent characteristics of personality, but by situational circumstances.[8] Psychologist Philip Zimbardo produced the most famous confirmation of the situational perspective in a 1971 experiment

Cindy Sherman, *Untitled Film Still #21*, 1978, black-and-white photograph, 30 x 40 inches. Like Patricia Hearst, Sherman was immersed in the issue of identity. For her *Untitled Film Still* series (1977–1981), she photographed herself in a variety of poses, postures, and costumes. Here, according to the Museum of Modern Art, "she is the pert young career girl in a trim new suit on her first day in the big city." Courtesy Cindy Sherman and Metro Pictures.

in which student volunteers acted out the roles of prisoners and guards in a "prison" constructed in the hallways of the Stanford psychology department. As Zimbardo later wrote, "The Evil Situation triumphed over the Good People." Within days, the guards had become sadists and many of the prisoners showed signs of extreme "emotional breakdown." "The prisoners who adapted better to the situation," Zimbardo reported—and here one cannot help but think of the kidnapped Patty Hearst—"were those who mindlessly followed orders and who allowed the guards to dehumanize and degrade them ever more with each passing day and night." The experiment had to be terminated after six days. Louis Jolyon West briefly mentioned the Zimbardo experiments during his testimony, and Bailey asked the court's permission (which was refused) to use in his closing argument a quotation from a textbook written by Zimbardo that included Patty Hearst as an example of brainwashing.[9]

From a broader perspective, historian and social critic Christopher Lasch argued in 1984 that the elements of a secure, stable selfhood—"a personal history, friends, family, a sense of place"—had been under siege. The result, and the title of his book, was "the minimal self." The existence of deep concerns with identity can also be read into the many efforts in the 1970s to locate and ground the self in time, place, and culture. These include such novels as Alex Haley's *Roots* (1976) and John Jakes's multivolume *Kent Family Chronicles* (1974–1979), and a burgeoning interest in historic preservation. Similarly, film critic Robert Kolker suggests that the "constant thematic" in the films of Martin Scorsese, arguably the most important filmic voice of the 1970s, was "the futile attempt to establish the self, to constitute subjectivity within a disinterested world."[10] Identity was also a regular theme of best-selling books of the decade, among them *Sybil* (1973), the story of a young woman tormented by sixteen selves or personalities, a condition the book claims was brought on by her parents: a powerful, insane mother and a distant father. Difficulty in achieving or reassembling a stable, cohesive identity can also be observed in Hollywood's post-1970 portrayal of the male therapist—the authoritative, patriarchal problem solver of earlier postwar films—as thoughtlessly arrogant (Leonard Nimoy in *Invasion of the Body Snatchers* [1978]); troubled (Bruce Willis in *Color of Night* [1994], Richard Gere in *Final Analysis* [1992]); or psychopathic (Anthony Hopkins's Dr. Hannibal Lecter in *The Silence of the Lambs* [1991]).Similarly, although films of the post-Vietnam era often featured soldiers and veterans traumatized by the conflict and by survivor guilt, the patriarchal, psychiatric solution of the post–World War II period (*Home of the Brave*, 1949) had by 1980 yielded to ongoing maladjustment (*The Deer Hunter*, 1978), a vortex of madness

(*Apocalypse Now*, 1979), and the rescue and revenge fantasies of *Uncommon Valor* (1983), *Missing in Action* (1984), and *Rambo: First Blood Part II* (1985).[11]

One also sees the fragile self mirrored in the two diseases most associated with the 1970s: Alzheimer's and anorexia nervosa. Public awareness of Alzheimer's, a dementia distinct from the normal processes of aging and with its own pathology, increased sharply, as did the prevalence of the disease, in the late 1960s and 1970s. It was understood as "the worst of all diseases," even as "the disease of the century," precisely because, as historian Jesse F. Ballenger has explained, it attacked qualities of personal responsibility and self-awareness that were at the core of what it meant to be a middle-class American. Perceptions of the disease were thus shaped by larger, contemporary concerns about the problematic nature of selfhood in a postmodern age; one might even say Alzheimer's emerged when and as it did because it so perfectly reflected both ubiquitous anxieties about the fragile self and the deep desire for its coherence and strength. "In modern America," writes Ballenger, "the emphasis on self-control through strength of will, self-creation through personal effort, and self-fulfillment through the creative and passionate pursuit of one's desires puts the social and moral status of the cognitively impaired in doubt."[12]

Anorexia was first identified as a disease in the 1870s, but its modern variant emerged a century later. What historian Joan Brumberg has called "the disease of the 1970s" entered the *Reader's Guide to Periodical Literature* as a category in 1974 and was a widely acknowledged social phenomenon long before 1983, when the popular singer and drummer Karen Carpenter died of the disease at age thirty-two. Without denying that anorexia was, indeed, a disease—a psychopathology—Brumberg, writing in 1988, argued that for many adolescent women the control of food and appetite was a way of using the body as a "symbolic language," a "vehicle for making a statement about their identity and personal dreams," a signifier of nonconsumption in a culture of affluence in which consumption and identity are powerfully linked: "In a sad and desperate way, today's fasting girls epitomize the curious psychic burdens of the dutiful daughters of a people of plenty." Although it may be inappropriate to describe anorexia as a lifestyle choice, a recent study of anorexics suggests how thoroughly the behaviors associated with the disease become linked with the identity of the victim. "It feels like my identity now," explained one young woman. "I suppose I worry that people don't know, they don't know the real me."[13]

At the highest level of academic discourse, the problem of the fragile self became marked in the 1970s by the concept of the narcissistic personality. Although "narcissism" was widely used in a simplistic way to describe what many commentators felt was a trend toward selfish behavior, the scholars who elevated the term to prominence in the decade—many of them psychiatrists—had something more complex in mind: a clinically defined personality disorder. Key elements of the narcissistic personality were a cold, unemotional self, distanced from family and society, unable to empathize or to appreciate others' emotional needs; feelings of anxiety, uncertainty, inner emptiness, and boredom; very low self-esteem coupled with a near-desperate need for approval, praise, and immediate gratification; a fragmented self and an inability to imagine personal coherence; delusions of grandeur and fantasies of self-importance, linked to desires to dominate; and compulsive anger and irritability leading to panic, thoughts of revenge, and moments of "narcissistic rage."[14]

For historian and social critic Christopher Lasch, the narcissistic personality was the product of long-term developments in Western society, including bureaucracy (encouraging people to think of themselves as role-players), the diminished importance of skilled work (with "personality" taking its place as the key to success), a declining faith in the sciences and in politics (making the future appear uncertain and bleak), the rise of an image-based society of celebrity and the spectacle (rendering everyday life boring and banal), the therapeutic outlook of modern medicine (promoting obsessions about health and appearance, and a view of life as survival), and, underlying everything else, a "general crisis of western culture" manifested as a "pervasive despair." The narcissist's "ideology of personal growth," Lasch concluded, is "the faith of those without faith."[15]

It is not difficult to understand how particular developments of the 1970s—an anemic economy, the Watergate scandal, the loss of control associated with the 1973 oil crisis and the beginnings of modern terrorism, signs of deindustrialization, the end of the progressive enthusiasm of the 1960s, the failure in Vietnam—intensified these long-term trends and deepened the flight to narcissism. But for Lasch and others, the most important mechanism for producing the narcissistic personality was the family. Weakened over the course of a century as its socializing functions were taken over by the state, the schools, the mass media, welfare services, and child-rearing experts, the family in the 1970s faced the additional challenge of a surging feminist movement whose adherents often seemed more interested in the workplace than in reproduction and child-rearing. At the family level, narcissism was seen as the result of parents' having lost the sense that they had something of importance to pass on to their children, of absent, inadequate fathers, and, especially, of cool, emotionally detached mothers more concerned with self-fulfillment than with their responsibilities to the next generation—"hiding," as Heinz Kohut put it, "behind bridge cards."[16]

Patty's relation to the modern, fragile self had several aspects. As Patricia Hearst, before the kidnapping, her identity problem was very different from the *absence* of family history and place that motivated Alex Haley to search for his past and that fueled the decade's enthusiasm for genealogy. Indeed, Patty suffered from a surfeit of family and place, with the weight of the Hearst name and San Simeon standing as obstacles to her quest for an authentic self. Aspects of her Berkeley lifestyle—the job at Capwell's, domestic life with Steven Weed—might be understood as efforts to lighten the burden of Hearst family history by dwelling in the ordinary; her 1979 marriage to a former bodyguard suggests that the effort was ongoing. In contrast, the SLA "offered" Patty a variety of new, intense forms of identity: a righteous political and social agenda; membership in a small group; a shared feminism; expertise in firearms; a harder, better conditioned body; the mysteries of the underground; a deviant sexuality; a dramatically heightened level of celebrity; the risks and titillations of life as a criminal. Which of these she accepted and valued, and to what degree, was the subject of her trial and remains controversial. In any case, it seems clear that the pleasures of identity were at play in Patty's SLA adventure, as they were for some of her companions. The day that Patty and her close friend, Wendy Yoshimura, were arrested, Wendy had written to a former lover about her experience with the SLA, foregrounding her own developing identity. "It was horrendous," she wrote, "but at the same time I've learned a hell of a lot. Now I understand more clearly my political views, and, oh, the sense of myself I've gotten out of this ordeal—I wouldn't exchange it for anything!" "I think most of us," she continued, in a reference that included Patty, "have come out ahead. I hope you'll have the chance to meet P. H. She is incredible!"[17] *Every Secret Thing* reveals a Patty who on some level enjoyed the radical reading regimen forced upon her by her relationship with the SLA, who took pride in her newly acquired expertise ("I could field-strip, put together, and load every gun in our arsenal"), and who may have taken some pleasure in her new body ("I could do shoulder rolls and crouches"), although she seems to have loathed jogging with weights and other painful exercises forced upon her by Bill and Emily Harris.[18]

The prosecution, of course, argued that Patty had fully taken on these new identities, and that she had done so not because of coercion from the SLA but—in part, at least—in rejection of

In the summer of 1974, the FBI used Patty's image from her photo with Steven Weed (see page 3) to create a series of composite images, each depicting her wearing a different wig. Together, they suggest what Patty had become, at last for some people: a set of curious identities or a young woman playing a series of roles. U.S. Department of Justice, Federal Bureau of Investigation, Record Group 65, National Archives.

her parents, especially her strong mother and her (relatively) weak father. Indeed, had it suited their case to do so, either side could have presented Patty as a young woman working out the substance of a narcissistic personality. Her parents fit the mold. Catherine, especially, matched the psychiatrists' description of the emotionally distant mother, having left the child Patty to an unyielding governess. At a crucial point after the kidnapping, she had appeared to put her career goals ahead of concern for Patty when she signed on for another term on the California Board of Regents. The "extended report" on Patty's condition by court-appointed psychiatrist Dr. Margaret Thaler Singer—not made available to the jury, but largely affirmed by testimony that was—resembled a primer on the narcissistic personality. One section, entitled "Uncertainty about Self," revealed a child unsure of parental love, doubting her self-worth, and, not long before the kidnapping, depressed at her lack of purpose. Other sections were entitled "Ambivalence Towards Her Parents," "Characterological Lack of Inner-Directedness," and "Psychological Suggestibility," the latter noting Patty's penchant for taking on the "ways of those around her." Although the narcissistic inclination to fits of rage better describes the conduct of Bill Harris, it might also explain Patty's indictment of her parents on the SLA tapes and in the "Tania Interview." In addition, the narcissist seeks fame and celebrity, and Patty's adventure with the SLA brought her plenty of both.[19]

Most of the scholars who have studied the Hearst event agree that Patty's complex, evolving identity was one of its central themes. Janice Schuetz's account suggests that each of Patty's names—Patty, Tania, and Pearl—corresponded to a different identity. "Patty" embodied Betty Friedan's "feminine mystique," "Tania" the SLA guerrilla, "Pearl" the radical feminist. And each of these self-definitions was influenced and shaped by other women: Catherine Hearst, the women of the SLA, Wendy Yoshimura.[20] While recognizing that Patty's identity underwent significant change as a result of her contact with the SLA, Christopher Castiglia celebrates Patty's new self and the discovery it represents: that the idea of a unified, unchanging self, he asserts, is itself a deception, a product of "discourses of power" whose purpose it is to insure that womanhood is understood as immutable.[21] Similarly, historian Andreas Killen suggests that

Patty's "conversion" to Tania was an extreme version of the attempts to "revolutionize" the self that proliferated in the 1970s, famously labeled by Tom Wolfe as "the Me Decade."[22]

This largely positive reading of Patty's changing self, emphasizing its subversive, antiauthoritarian possibilities, suggests a cultural link with punk rock and its New York scene, whose emergence is often dated to the opening of the underground club CBGB to punk productions in March 1974, not long after Patty was abducted. Patty's transformation, and the various punk approaches to music and fashion, were intended in part as critiques of fossilized, banal modes of middle-class existence and as assertions of the possibility of throwing off the conditioning of the dominant culture. Both movements had collective elements, reflected in Patty's transformation from the highly individualized Patty Hearst to the SLA soldier Tania, and in the desire of the Ramones and other bands to create a democratic, participatory rock scene. Reflecting on the contribution of the New York scene, Richard Hell of the band Television emphasized his desire to restore to rock n' roll "the knowledge that you invent yourself. That's why I changed my name, why I did all the clothing style things, haircut, everything. . . . If you just amass the courage that is necessary, you can completely invent yourself. You can be your own hero."[23]

In contrast, Nancy Isenberg presents Patty's evolving and overlapping "simulated" identities as an instance of postmodern pastiche and manipulation, orchestrated by the SLA (rather than chosen by Patty) as a form of guerrilla theater reminiscent of the 1960s and intended to challenge bourgeois concepts of individuality and socialization. "The SLA," she writes, "was deliberately displaying how easily an individual could adopt a new identity, a radically different gender script of behavior." Uncomfortable with this multiplicity and complexity, the jurors, Isenberg argues, preferred "to imagine a whole Patty Hearst," and they believed they had found it in the Cujo/Tania romance, which at once made Patty a liar and a woman they could understand.[24] On a cultural level, the jurors' discomfort with Patty's multiple identities, and their desire to understand her as "whole," was analogous to the contemporary concerns about Alzheimer's and attitudes toward its sufferers. For the jurors and the public, the brainwashed/multiple Patty and the Alzheimer's patient were similarly diseased—both "cognitively impaired," both deprived of the coherence, strength of will, and self-control that loomed so large as essential human traits in the late twentieth century.[25]

In addition to a growing academic interest in the fragile and besieged self, the 1970s witnessed the emergence or efflorescence of threats to the modern, unmoored personality, some of them "real," some fantasies circulating in the popular culture, some based on recent developments in the sciences tinged with a futuristic flavor. Among the most prominent of these threats was the "cult," a pejorative usually reserved for religious groups outside the mainstream, whose members were often seen as being in thrall to a charismatic male leader, ready to overwhelm—to program—the vulnerable. Consciousness of cults increased dramatically in the late 1960s and 1970s, in response to the Manson family murders, the growth of Hare Krishna and the Unification Church (also known as the Moonies, after its leader, the Reverend Sun Myung Moon, whose Korean background evoked memories of Korean War POWs and the chilling sequences involving brainwashed veterans in the 1962 movie *The Manchurian Candidate*), and the 1978 mass suicide in Guyana of members of the Peoples Temple and its leader, Jim Jones. Margaret Singer, the cult expert and clinical psychologist whose report on Patty Hearst never reached the jury, estimated that by the late 1970s there were at least 250 cults in the United States, including satanic and witchcraft-based movements, race-based groups, communal living associations, and believers in flying saucers.[26]

Although the Symbionese Liberation Army was seldom described as a cult, the Manson "family"—a recognized cult—was a frequent point of reference during the trial and in the press. Both Manson's family and the SLA were heavily female, each centered on a dominant male—a figure who for many was the solution to what was increasingly understood as the nation's crisis of patriarchal authority. (Ronald Reagan would play a similar role politically.) The SLA's efforts to convert Patty resembled those used by (other) cults, and Cinque's presence and style, combined with the adulation he demanded from Bill Harris and others, suggests that the SLA could reasonably be taken as an example of what Singer called a "race-based" cult. Cinque and Harris exhibited the "wild travesties of patriarchal authority" that Killen identifies with Manson, Moon, and Lyndon LaRouche, cult figures who responded to the social instability of the late 1960s and early 1970s with fantasies of male dominance.[27]

Patty's sense of a stable self was also affected by changing configurations of celebrity. Of course, Patty was a celebrity long before the kidnapping; as a Hearst, she qualified for that status under historian Daniel Boorstin's iconic definition of the celebrity as "*a person who is known for his well-knownness*"—although, as we have seen, she was uncomfortable in that role and had made modest efforts, including a plain lifestyle in Berkeley, to avoid the spotlight. After the kidnapping, Patty was caught up in what Lasch and Todd Gitlin describe as a new kind of theatrical, image-based political celebrity, based on the merging of "politics and spectacle." Practiced by presidents John F. Kennedy and Richard Nixon as "crisis management," the practice was translated in the late 1960s and early 1970s by elements of the New Left into a sensational, media-centered politics of confrontation, style, rhetoric, symbolism—and celebrity—which emphasized a sort of guerrilla theater and served to personalize a group's political or social agenda. For Lasch and Gitlin, the perverse and pathetic culmination of this trend was Patty's kidnapping by the SLA, a group ungrounded in any significant constituency yet determined to personalize and market its rhetoric and ideology.[28]

Functioning as a marketing agency, the SLA used Patty's taped statements to push its message onto the airwaves and into a rapidly growing mass print medium, exemplified by *People* magazine, founded in 1974 to "focus entirely on the active personalities of our time," and by *Newsweek*, a traditional weekly tempted by the celebrity business and unable to resist putting Patty's image on its cover. The SLA's publicity project also benefited from—and helped create—intense interest in what media scholar Ellis Cashmore calls the "plasticity of people": the question of why people do what they do, and how one could be made to do something that seems foreign to one's normal behavior or proclivities. Those issues, fundamental to Patty's experience and to the public's reception of it, were being explored in psychology by Zimbardo and by Stanley Milgram (discussed below); in holocaust studies; in films as diverse as *The Machurian Candidate* and the 1978 version of *Invasion of the Body Snatchers*; and, as Cashmore notes, in the 1973 television drama *An American Family*, featuring the Louds, a real family that came unglued in our living rooms. In retrospect, the Louds were celebrities of a new sort, the pioneers of reality TV, ordinary people living Andy Warhol's 1968 prediction: "In the future, everyone will be world-famous for 15 minutes."[29]

Patty's celebrity was of an impure variety, a curious mixture of types: heiress, crime victim, mass-media spectacle, reality-show participant, and (according to the prosecution) gun-toting bank robber. Unlike Madonna, who gave herself to commodification, or the contestants on *American Idol*, who hunger for any chance at fame, Patty could not avoid certain aspects of her celebrity, including the Hearst name and the kidnapping. Other aspects of her notoriety—her image as a bank robber, as a fugitive, as a revolutionary, as a woman with a gun—may have been "chosen," or at least not fully and forcefully rejected. The jury thought so. To suggest that possibility is to acknowledge that Patty was a player in a celebrity culture that offered minor celebrities (like Patty) and non-celebrities (like the Loud family) a tempting variety of possible new high-profile identities, not all of them risk-free.

One risk—a risk that Patty clearly understood as she grappled early on with the consequences of the Hearst name—was that celebrity inevitably brings with it a loss of control over the content of the self, as celebrity followers and "fans" with their own concerns seek to shape the behavior of the celebrity or to understand the celebrity in ways that serve their personal needs and interests. For example, in Hollywood's golden age, movie fans sought influence over the stars and studios, threatening to boycott particular films, exposing the lies and half-truths of the industry publicity machines, withdrawing support from arrogant stars, or seeking to influence the casting of films. Patty was no film star (not yet, anyway), and there were, one assumes, no Patty Hearst fan clubs, but few Americans were without an opinion of Patty's actions and choices, and a wide range of their views could be found on the editorial and op-ed pages of the daily newspapers. Patty would have feedback.[30]

What people expect from celebrities varies from era to era, and the expectations of Patty's public were specific to the 1970s. Generally speaking, at the root of the fascination with celebrity is what Stuart Ewen calls "the dream of identity." The celebrity, no longer an ordinary person, offers ordinary people, through a bond of identification, the possibility of visibility, a hope of transcendence. In *The Image* (1960), his influential study of celebrity, Daniel Boorstin contrasted the big name, the empty celebrity of our age, produced through marketing, with the big man, the self-made hero of the past. In the absence of genuine heroes, people would ask mere celebrities to do the cultural work of great men—a request doomed, Boorstin argued, by the limited strengths and talents of the modern celebrity. But Patty's complex, multivalent celebrity opened up possibilities not available with say, Fabian or Paris Hilton or, to name a celebrity flavor of the 1970s, Nadia Comaneci. Patty could be understood as celebrity and as heroine, made and self-made, media fiction and real woman, victim and agent. Her burden—a burden on her self—was that the public demanded resolution and clarity. They wanted Patty to decide.[31]

Another challenge to the self came from the sciences, where emerging and nascent technologies—computers, robotics, cybernetics, genetics, and behavioral engineering (including brainwashing/coercive persuasion)—threatened to circumscribe the free individual and to make human beings something less than fully human. Many of these widely expressed concerns came together in *The Stepford Wives*, a 1975 science fiction film based on a 1972 novel, in which the husbands of suburban Stepford Village—inspired by the uncomplicated pleasures of consumerism, the simulacra of Disneyland, the airbrushed photos in *Playboy*, and an odd desire for a life without idiosyncrasy—find a way to replace their demanding wives with sexually provocative robots dedicated to cooking and cleaning. The technical expertise for this project comes from corporate America. In the movie, the town is full of high-tech companies specializing in electronics, computers, and aerospace; the book foregrounds a different set of technologies (systems engineering, vinyl polymers, microcircuitry, optical sensing) and names as coconspirators, the developers of "audioanimatronics" at Disneyland—the people who made the presidential figures talk. The evil men of Stepford Village do not attempt to solve their "problem" with genetics, perhaps because the last thing they want is to produce exact copies of their spouses. But even in 1975 they likely would have been aware of that science's manipulative potential; English scientists had cloned a frog in 1968, and with that achievement came the knowledge—uncomfortable for many—that the genetic engineering of a human being was, in theory, possible.[32]

One element of the Stepford tale—the victimization of middle-class white women by a male establishment—was present in a drug epidemic/panic that had begun in the late 1960s with concerns about the widespread use of amphetamines and barbiturates but peaked in the mid-1970s, with the sedative Valium at center stage. As described by historian David Herzberg, this panic was distinctive because its addicts were respectable, middle-class, upper-middle-class, and wealthy people, predominantly women. By the end of the decade, former first lady Betty Ford had revealed herself to be a Valium user, and the dimensions of the problem had been probed, studied, and publicized by the American Medical Association, consumer advocate Ralph Nader, advice columnist Ann Landers, the television news program *60 Minutes*, feminist Betty Friedan, and a Senate committee chaired by Edward Kennedy. Among the issues raised by the controversy were several evocative of the Patty Hearst saga. Like Patty's "conversion" and subsequent militance, the Valium epidemic raised the possibility that millions of women were less than satisfied with their traditional roles as housewives, mothers, and consumers and might seek to change what had been presumed to be their immutable identities. And because many of the Valium users were white and well-to-do—again, like Patty—their addiction threatened the middle-class sense of invulnerability, the belief that social problems emerged from, and remained with, the "other." The slogan "she could even be you" had its origins in the drug panic, but it expressed a concern also voiced in the context of the Hearst case.[33]

The changing rhetoric of the Valium episode likewise paralleled changes in the way Patty's conduct was understood and evaluated. In the mid-1960s, Herzberg explains, "addiction" connoted "a disease rather than a criminal act." The drug user was thus defined as a victim (of the drug's properties, or the prescribing physician, or both). Similarly, the core of F. Lee Bailey's defense of Patty Hearst was to present his client as an unwilling victim of a brutal kidnapping. The understanding of addiction as a disease remained prevalent into the 1970s, but by 1980 addicts were increasingly being held personally responsible for their plight, and "she could even be you" had morphed into Nancy Reagan's "Just Say No."[34] This view of the drug user resembled the government's case against Patty Hearst, which asserted that Patty's criminal activity had flowed from conscious decisions and her free will.

Also suggestive of the fragile self was the theme of possession, well represented in films of the era. To be "possessed" was to lose control of one's self, one's soul, to some external force—usually the devil. The most critically acclaimed and influential of the possession films was *The Exorcist* (1973), which did very well at the box office, peaking at about the time Patty was kidnapped. The victim of possession here is Regan MacNeil (Linda Blair), a girl not unlike Patty: normal, kind, more than a little pampered, lacking deep religious beliefs, living a life of affluence, her father absent. Like Patty, Regan might be said to lack the inner resources—strength of self, solid grounding in a two-parent family and a real community, integrity of purpose—she would need to resist possession. Patty was frequently depicted as a spoiled "sixties" brat, while Regan's name evokes the cruel and grasping second daughter in Shakespeare's *King Lear*. *The Exorcist* ushered in a spate of possession films, including *Burnt Offerings* and *Cathy's Cause* (both 1976), *Audrey Rose*, *Good against Evil*, and *God Told Me To* (1977), *Amityville Horror* and *The Omen* (1979), and *Possession* (1981). Although Patty never claimed that the devil made her rob the Hibernia Bank, the idea that she might somehow have been possessed was never far from the surface. Indeed, Shana Alexander described the trial as a "form of twentieth-century exorcism." However, prosecution witness Joel Fort, talking with Alexander after the trial, dismissed the comparison: "The simpleminded notion that 'brainwashing' can account for complex behavior such as this defendant engaged in is no better an explanation than possession by the devil used to be."[35]

If Patty was seldom said to be possessed, she was frequently described as a "zombie." Alexander used the term often to describe the defendant's pallid, low-affect appearance in the courtroom, and ultimately found this perception of Patty deeply disturbing. "If she were a zombie," Alexander concluded in a curious use of the therapeutic voice, "I could not help her." Indeed, as a viewer of any zombie film would know, zombies are not present (whether in the movies or in our imaginations) to be helped; they can only be killed, and that with difficulty. Yet they do have characteristics. Writing in 1965, when the zombie phenomenon was in its infancy, Susan Sontag described the qualities of "emotionlessness, of impersonality, of regimentation" that characterized the "zombie-like" invaders common to science fiction films of the 1950s. Director George Romero's zombie trilogy—*Night of the Living Dead* (1968), *Dawn of the Dead* (1978), and *Day of the Dead* (1985)—offers insight into the zombie and, one should add, into contemporary anxieties about the nature of humanity, anxieties expressed and heightened in the mid-1970s by the figure of Patty Hearst.[36]

Zombies lack an inner existence, an elemental human consciousness; they are creatures of rote habit, bereft of agency; they exist only in the present, functioning without a sense of past or future; they are driven only by the most primitive instincts of survival; and, by the late 1970s, they carry a deadly contagion. "Zombies," writes film scholar Peter Dendle, "are people reduced to the lowest common denominator. The zombie is simply the hulk, the rude stuff of generic humanity, the bare canvas; passion, art, and intellect are by implication reduced to mere ornament. . . . The zombie just is." The zombie is, to be sure, a victim, but a victim beyond therapy and beyond redemption.[37]

The fear that human beings are vulnerable creatures, rather easily drained of the basic qualities of humanness, was amply displayed in *Invasion of the Body Snatchers*, the well-received 1978 remake of the iconic 1956 original. Creatures from outer space have arrived in idyllic San Francisco in the form of lovely flowers and their spores, producing huge pods that "clone" (and kill) sleeping earthlings, creating a new race, identical in appearance to the old one but, like zombies, lacking emotive qualities. "Something's missing," Elizabeth Driscoll (Brooke Adams) says of her boyfriend, who has been "changed." "Emotion. Feelings. He's just not the same person."

Driscoll and Matthew Bennell (Donald Sutherland) are the protagonists of this dark drama, but two more minor characters provide its analytical core. One is Nancy Bellicec (Veronica Cartwright), the only one of the main characters to remain unchanged at the end of the film, though that status is about to end. Her longevity appears to arise from her links to the 1960s counterculture; she's married to an iconoclast poet, and she operates a combination mud-bath and massage parlor.

The other character, with considerably more screen time, is Dr. David Kibner, an overbearing psychiatrist and author who responds to Elizabeth's fears with therapeutic psychobabble—"Will you trust me?" "All I'm trying to do is help"—of the sort that the Hearst jury found unconvincing. While everyone else has to be cloned to lose his or her humanity, Kibner is a smug, low-affect rationalist from the beginning, a rock of tempered reason (albeit wrong) in a sea of fear and speculation. Kibner is played by Leonard Nimoy, who had perfected the hyperrational role as First Officer Spock in seventy-nine episodes of the television series *Star Trek* (1966–1969). His most important scene takes place after Driscoll and Bennell have been captured. Kibner, now "changed," injects both with a sedative intended to speed their own cloning. "You'll be born again," he explains, "into an untroubled world. Free of anxiety, fear, hate. . . . There's no need for hate now, or love. . . . Don't be trapped by old concepts. You're evolving into a new life form." These few, brief lines touch on several prominent issues of the decade: the decline of the 1960s counterculture, represented especially by the word "love," strongly identified with the San Francisco summer of 1967; the emerging religious right; and the sense that Americans, in flight from the social and cultural upheavals of the 1960s, could be tempted to seek comfort—mere survival, mere existence—in an "untroubled world." Of course, viewers of the film detested Kibler's smarmy call for acquiescence and applauded Driscoll's and Bennell's futile efforts at flight and resistance. They had expected no less from Patty Hearst.

The Victim

The logic of the fragile self led to Patty-as-victim. If Patty was, like the rest of us, weak and vulnerable, and subject to a new technology of persuasion—brainwashing, or coercive persuasion—then how could she be blamed for anything: for being attracted to some of the ideas of the SLA, for joining the movement, for robbing a bank, for being paranoid, for not having tried to escape, for being "possessed"? For the most part, Bailey had advanced this argument, relying heavily on psychiatry, a discipline that openly acknowledged its ties to determinism. Psychiatrists perceive that free will is "a fiction," said forensic psychiatrist Dr. Seymour Pollack in 1974 testimony to a Senate committee holding hearings on criminal law reform. "Many psychiatrists, therefore, are opposed to criminal actors being punished under criminal law." In contrast, the "law," in the words of jurist Roscoe Pound, "postulates a free agent confronted with a choice of doing right and doing wrong and choosing freely to do wrong." "Lawyers and psychiatrists," summarized Karl Menninger in 1968, "speak two different languages."[38]

Just how much weight should be given in criminal proceedings to extralegal matters was in the 1970s very much a live issue. Court decisions in the 1950s had established that mental disease or defect could render a person not criminally responsible for an act, and that a defendant suffering from an "uncontrollable compulsion" was not a "free agent." By the early 1970s, some legal authorities believed that factors such as racial discrimination and poverty ought also to be taken as mitigating, and William Ryan, in his widely read book *Blaming the Victim* (1971), cautioned against what he observed as a growing tendency to fix responsibility for poverty, the slums, and other problems in some social pathology of the damaged. Patty was a victim, too—of kidnapping and coercive persuasion at least—and had the Hearst case been decided in Patty's favor on that ground, it would have chipped away further at the "law" and its confidence in the existence and relevance of free will.[39]

The history of the idea of the victim remains to be written, but two recent books offer insight into a concept that was at the center of the Hearst defense until Bailey changed course in his summation. Kirsten Fermaglich's *American Dreams and Nazi Nightmares* (2006) examines the work of four American Jewish scholars who published influential studies in the late 1950s and early 1960s: historian Stanley Elkins, feminist Betty Friedan, psychologist Stanley Milgram, and psychiatrist Robert Jay Lifton (who testified at the Hearst trial). Each of them drew on the twentieth century's quintessential experience of victimization—the Holocaust, carried out in Nazi concentration camps—to explain aspects of American society. In *Slavery* (1959), Elkins used the analogy of the concentration camp to explain black slavery. Like Friedan and Lifton, Elkins was deeply influenced by the perspective of Holocaust survivor Bruno Bettelheim, summarized in *The Informed Heart* (1960), in which the camps were understood to be places of vast and complete dehumanization, where the absence of privacy, control over bodily functions including eating and defecation, and the ever-present fear of death inevitably produced infantilization, emasculation, and the disintegration of the personality. Similarly, Elkins argued, the "closed" system of slavery, amplifying its power and control and severely restricting opportunities for slaves to exercise authority even within the family, had reduced even the most heroic, warlike, and individualistic male slaves to passive, childlike servants of their masters—that is, to mere victims, profoundly damaged.[40]

Friedan, whose *The Feminine Mystique* (1963) was an immediate best-seller, used the same analogy to describe the tragedy that had befallen suburban women, turning many of them into "dependent, passive, childlike," parasitic victims of the "comfortable concentration camp[s]" that were their suburban homes. "The women who 'adjust' as housewives, who grow up wanting to be 'just a housewife,'" she wrote, "are in as much danger as the millions who walked to their own death in the concentration camps."[41]

By employing the concentration camp analogy, Elkins and Friedan foregrounded the enormous power that closed, totalizing systems—the concentration camp, the slave plantation, the suburban home environment—brought to bear on their respective inmates. But what of the other side of the equation? What about the human being, the person, ensnared by a closed and dominant system? Is victimhood inevitable, or do people possess qualities that would allow them to resist or transcend these difficult environments? Friedan, Milgram, and Lifton offered rather pessimistic responses. For Friedan, "aspects of the housewife role . . . make it almost impossible for a woman of adult intelligence to retain a sense of human identity, the firm core of self or 'I' without which a human being, man or woman, is not truly alive." Yet the roots of what Friedan labeled "today's identity crisis" went deeper than the housewife role or the restrictive suburban home, deeper even than the society's limiting and confining ideas of gender. The fragile, vulnerable self that the suburban woman presented to the world was, Friedan argued, a product of a society of abundance, in which most people—men as well as women—are deprived of meaningful, fulfilling, purposeful *work*. Friedan did not claim that this was a new problem; indeed, she argued that it was at least a century old. But the ideology of the "feminine mystique" had made postwar women blind to the problem of work and, for those who had vision, disinclined to take action. American women, she concluded, were "faced with the slow death of self," consigned—like the zombies they resembled—to a "living death."[42]

Consistent with the concept of the vulnerable, victimized self that they had observed in the Nazi concentration camps, Milgram and Lifton explored the contours of the malleable persona. Both were interested in explaining the circumstances under which the self could be changed and transformed: Milgram was preoccupied with the problem of how ordinary people could be turned into killers, as Adolf Eichmann and other ordinary Germans had been; Lifton with the transformation of the adult personality under the stress of "extreme situations," a term used by Bettelheim in his study of the concentration camps. In what became known as the "obedience" experiments, carried out at Yale University in the early 1960s and first published in 1963, Milgram demonstrated that a high percentage of naïve subjects, told that they were participants in a study of the effect of punishment on learning, could, under stress, be made to administer what they believed to be very painful electric shocks to "students" who provided "incorrect" answers. He concluded that human beings involved in hierarchical structures are naturally obedient. Lifton's scholarship covered a much broader range of ideas, from brainwashing and Chinese thought reform to the idea of the traumatized "survivor" (the source for the concept of "post-traumatic stress disorder"). Like Elkins and Friedan, his research focused on victims—inmates of the concentration camps, survivors of Hiroshima, veterans of the war in Vietnam—although his emphasis on the "survivors" of these traumas gave his work a somewhat more optimistic tone. Like Milgram, he came to believe that identity was unstable, that the self was always in flux, and that the adult personality could be rather quickly and easily transformed, especially in Bettelheim's "extreme situations."[43]

The most important contributions of this group of scholars—the consciousness of the Holocaust that they brought to their respective inquiries, the focus on victims of extreme situations, the malleable self that emerged from their studies—were products of a particular historical period, the turn of the 1960s, when a particular kind of liberalism, characterized by concerns about racism, the nuclear bomb, and the impact of mass society on individuals, allowed these ideas to germinate and, in the decade to come, to flourish. By the mid-1970s—when Patty was on trial—this formulation of the concept of the victim had lost some of its appeal. In 1976 Elkins's *Slavery*, which had sold 330,000 copies since its first publication, went into a final printing. Taking its place was John W. Blassingame's *The Slave Community: Plantation Life in the Antebellum South* (1972), a transitional work that recognized the power of "total" institutions, especially the concentration camp, to produce dependent, docile, childlike behavior, yet argued that the plantation, despite its cruelties, offered slaves the physical and psychological space necessary to maintain self-esteem and group solidarity. Far from having been transformed into blindly obedient Sambos, the slaves Blassingame described held onto a desire for freedom, hated all whites, engaged in acts of disobedience and rebellion, and employed deference as a ritual and tactic that disguised their true feelings and attitudes. *The Slave Community* signaled the emergence of a revisionist perspective on the slave experience, one emphasizing resistance rather than passive victimization, and it reflected a similar shift in thinking about the Jewish experience in the concentration camps. In October 1976 some five hundred people attended a special session at the annual meeting of the Association for the Study of Afro-American Life and History, dedicated to discussion of *The Slave Community* and its provocative argument about human behavior in captivity. At the time, Patty had been in prison for one month.[44]

In contrast, Friedan's *The Feminine Mystique* remained popular throughout the 1970s, riding the wave of feminism. But the victim-based phrase "comfortable concentration camps," which had received much favorable attention in the 1960s, was seldom noted in the decade that followed, as feminism too turned from its focus on passive, psychologically damaged victims. Indeed, as early as 1973, some feminists were using the term "victim" negatively. At the same time, Milgram's obedience experiments came under attack from those unwilling to accept his claim that most people were capable of Eichmann-like evil. Marking his own turn to the right, New York intellectual Daniel Bell argued that Milgram's position undermined individual responsibility. A similar critique from the right would be leveled at Lifton's concept of post–traumatic stress disorder, but by and large Lifton's treatment of the victim remained viable longer, perhaps because of an upbeat connotation of the word "survivor," as in "I am not a victim. I am a survivor."[45]

Among those not asked to participate in Patty's trial, no name looms larger than that of B. F. Skinner, the behavioral psychologist. It was not that Skinner's work was irrelevant to Patty's situation; indeed, one scholar of the Nazi concentration camps argued in the mid-1970s that Skinnerian behaviorism was at the forefront of "the case for man-as-victim" because it assumed "outright that environment is omnipotent and that the human self is ever and always a unilateral function of the world in which it finds itself."[46] Rather, Skinner had always been a polarizing figure, and increasingly so after the publication in 1971 of his best-selling *Beyond Freedom and Dignity*. Deeply concerned for the survival of mankind in a global world characterized by environmental pollution, overpopulation, declining resources, and the threat of nuclear holocaust, Skinner advocated social arrangements built, modified, and improved through the science of behavioral engineering. This would be possible only, he believed, if people dispensed with the false idea that humans were conscious, autonomous beings, possessing dignity and free to make decisions—and therefore responsible for the decisions they made. "In the traditional view," Skinner wrote, "a person is free. He is autonomous in the sense that his behavior is uncaused" (anticipating the prosecution's characterization of Patty as a "rebel in search of a cause"). "He can therefore be held responsible for what he does and justly punished if he offends. That view," Skinner concluded, "must be re-examined." Reexamination required abandoning a whole range of "pre-scientific" ways of explaining human behavior, from human nature and traits of character to "intentions, purposes, aims, and goals." Here was the fragile self in the extreme: the inner being, feeling and emotions, attitudes, personality, the soul, will—all illusions. "Psychology," as one writer put it, "without a psyche."[47] For Skinner, environment was everything, and guilt—Patty's guilt, for example—was an absurdity.

As attractive as this perspective must have been to those charged with defending Patty Hearst and explaining her behavior (or that of anyone else), Bailey rightly distanced his client from a position that was not only controversial but under attack. One group of critics argued that Skinner's desire for a predictable world based on behavioral engineering had blinded him to what was novel and unpredictable not only in human behavior but in the realm of science. Historian Paul F. Boller Jr. insisted that Beethoven, Marx, Freud, and others were "surely more than the sum total of the positive and negative reinforcers making up their lives." Similarly, social critic and historian Richard Sennett claimed that Skinner's approach ignored quantum mechanics' Heisenberg uncertainty principle, according to which matter behaved unpredictably. Several writers took issue with Skinner's dismissal of emotion and consciousness. Writing in *Natural History*, Spencer Klaw argued that "any science of human behavior that cannot—or does not choose to—penetrate this realm seems so incomplete as to be, at best, of limited value in ordering our affairs." Looking back on his own prominent career as a humanistic psychologist, Carl T. Rogers took up Skinner's behaviorist challenge, insisting that "man is to some degree the architect of himself." In *American Psychologist*, Herbert M. Lefcourt took the position that freedom (like control) *was* an illusion, but a useful one with consequences, perhaps even "the bedrock on which life flourishes."[48] Criticism came from both sides of the political spectrum. From the left came accusations that Skinner's approach was undemocratic and elitist, even fascist; in the *Atlantic Monthly*, George Kateb suggested that in his desire to "undermine the practice of praise and blame" Skinner was "casting out the language of judgment" and pushing social relations toward the atrophied Newspeak of *1984*. Predictably, the libertarian right also found fault. Ayn Rand wrote critically of Skinner's work, and the Intercollegiate Studies Institute, an academic arm of the libertarian movement, eventually placed *Beyond Freedom and Dignity* on its list "The Fifty Worst Books of the [Twentieth] Century."[49]

By the mid-1970s, then, when Patty went on trial, the Holocaust-inspired, turn-of-the-1960s liberal idea of the helpless victim, while still vital, had come under siege, mostly from the right. Alyson M. Cole's *The Cult of True Victimhood: From the War on Welfare to the War on Terror* (2007), confirms that turn while presenting the broader outlines of a modern history of the concept of the victim. Cole demonstrates that the antivictimist position was not fully realized until the 1990s, with the publication of a spate of books, many of them inspired by distaste for the welfare state, affirmative action, identity politics, feminism, and other phenomena associated with the "radical" 1960s. The critique reached the popular culture in the film *The Accused* (1988), in which a raped woman, played by Jody Foster, is denied the status of victim and accused of having brought on the act, and *Dangerous Minds* (1995), in which Michelle Pfeiffer's teacher character announces, "There are no victims in this class!"[50]

It seems clear then, that the antivictimist impulses at work in the 1970s, while real enough, were but the opening salvos in what would become an all-out war. Even so, that decade saw real and consequential changes, as Patty would learn when the verdict was read. One pivotal event was the publication in 1971 of William Ryan's *Blaming the Victim*. Ryan was a committed liberal, and he believed that there were, indeed, victims—

people who had been victimized by economic and social processes, along Marxist lines. As Cole makes clear, however, *Blaming the Victim* was a transitional book, a way station between the turn-of-the-1960s ideas of Friedan and Elkins and the later, conservative hostility to victimism. While acknowledging the economic and social *causes* of victimization, Ryan refused to characterize his victims as passive, dependent, or pathologically damaged. He refused, that is, to focus on the *character* of the victim. He refused to "blame the victim."[51]

By the mid-1970s, victimology had become a recognized field of study, with its own conferences and journal—a sign of a vital field of inquiry in which fundamental issues remained unresolved. While a strong feminist movement insisted that raped women were victims, pure and simple, and a victims' rights movement and calls for "affirmation action" for victims continued to gain traction, antivictimists stressed "character building," "personal responsibility," and variations on Lifton's "survivor," a term that could connote, as Cole has written, "the victim's journey, her progress up from victimhood."[52]

The Survivor

Perhaps sensing that the jury would be unwilling to pioneer a new role for psychiatry in the criminal law and unreceptive to arguments that followed a strict victimist line of reasoning, Bailey in his closing argument nearly abandoned what until then had been critical elements of Patty's defense: brainwashing or coercive persuasion, and the testimony of psychiatrists. Instead, as we have seen, he reconstituted the idea of survival.

By about 1970, survival was emerging as an important cultural concept, with several very different meanings. One version, presented by defense witness Robert Jay Lifton, centered on the "survivor syndrome," a psychiatric term that marked survival as akin to an illness. In this formulation, Patty was a victim of a process of coercive persuasion that had effectively destroyed her sense of self and reduced her to a state of total compliance with the demands of the SLA. Until Bailey's closing argument, that, in essence, was Patty's defense: the survivor as victim.

The powerlessness at the core of the survivor/victim concept resonated in the 1970s with a relatively new theory of human actions and behavior that was rooted in biology. The biological perspective had emerged full-blown in the 1960s with the publication of Robert Ardrey's *African Genesis* (1961), Desmond Morris's *The Naked Ape* (1967), and many works of scholarship that emphasized the animal nature of the human species and the legacy of biologically programmed irrationality that seemed to flow from it, while minimizing the role of conscious systems of decision making.[53]

Although the biological approach was a good fit for a disillusioned era in which many problems appeared intractable and survival seemed a necessary and sufficient goal, its emergence did not go uncontested. While acknowledging the truth of evolution, Dr. Benjamin Spock introduced the 1977 edition of *Baby and Child Care* by emphasizing the ways in which humans were different from animals. "Our relationships are predominantly spiritual," he wrote, and "our capacity for abstract reasoning has enabled us to discover much of the meaning of the universe." Writing in William Buckley's right-wing *National Review*, Gerhart Niemeyer also took issue with biology's portrait of a humanity governed by base instincts. "Man is dignified," he wrote, "inasmuch as he has been given reason and the power to distinguish right from wrong."[54]

More recently, psychologists who study the brain have recast the basic biological dichotomy while retaining its essential features. In this recasting, human animality is presented as a powerful, dominant "automatic system," shaped by natural selection and serving to respond quickly and reliably to pleasure and pain and to "trigger survival-related motivations," along with a less powerful "controlled system" that seeks to apply conscious, rational thought processes to human behavior. Psychologist Jonathan Haidt describes this system through the metaphor of the elephant (the dominant, emotion-based, automatic system) and the rider (the conscious, controlled system). The rider, Haidt concludes, is "placed on the elephant's back to help the elephant make better choices . . . but the rider cannot order the elephant around against its will."[55]

Imagine, then, Patty Hearst—kidnapped, bruised, caged, blindfolded, raped, threatened with death—dealing with her pain and fear by simply being the animal she was, her "elephant" in total control, ignoring its "rider," calling on eons of evolutionary experience to produce the decisions that were most likely to result in survival. Shorn of the explicit biological references, that was, in Bailey's closing argument, Patty's defense. The government, the jury, and most Americans apparently preferred the Spock/Niemeyer vision of human nature. They wanted Patty's rider to turn the elephant around.

Another, somewhat more upbeat idea of survival—one might label it "muddling through"—also circulated in the 1970s. It articulated the sense that many Americans had that they were survivors of one disaster or another—even, one might say, the sense that they were living through a disastrous era that defined life as survivorship. For perhaps most Americans, surviving the 1970s meant getting by, somehow coping with waves of factory closings, skyrocketing gasoline prices and home heating bills, a stagnant stock market, and rising rates of divorce and single parenting. "Amid the wreckage," writes Andreas Killen, "Americans discovered that instead of a chosen people they had become a nation of survivors."[56]

Hollywood's contribution to this notion of the survivor can be found in Tony Manero and Bud Davis, the rather unremarkable characters played by John Travolta in *Saturday Night Fever* (1977) and *Urban Cowboy* (1980). Both Manero and Davis work by day for a modicum of nighttime glory, playing the game of survival while cautiously exploring a netherworld of moderate risk. *Saturday Night Fever*'s hit song, sung by the Bee Gees and appropriately titled "Stayin' Alive," contains a couplet that sums up the limited expectations of Manero and many in the film's audience: "You know it's all right, it's OK / I'll live to see another day."[57]

This conception of survival was accompanied by a decline in the dream of collective social action; one muddled through alone, or at best with small groups of marginalized, like-minded others. In the 1960s, the great tasks of the age had been accomplished collectively, with other students who wanted to end the war in Vietnam, other poor people linked in welfare rights organizations, other liberals willing to march on Washington to achieve racial integration. By the mid-1970s, confidence that such large networks of reform could be built and made useful was crumbling. With notable exceptions that included the women's rights and gay rights movements, social action gravitated to political splinter groups such as the Weathermen (and the SLA); to cultlike organizations such as Jim Jones's Peoples Temple, that chose to withdraw from society rather than find accommodation or seek political change; and to frustrated and angry individuals, dependent on their own resources. At one end of the spectrum, the transition from group to individual can be observed in something as simple as the breakup of the Beatles, with their tight, cohesive sound and the sense of community it evoked, and the subsequent emergence of Paul McCartney as an individual star (on "The Lovely Linda," an ode to his wife on his self-titled 1970 album, McCartney plays all the parts himself).

At the other end of the spectrum are the communitarian fantasies, exemplified on-screen by bank robber Sonny Wortzik (Al Pacino) in *Dog Day Afternoon* (1975), whose cries of "Attica! Attica!" serve only to reveal his distance from the hopeful, collective politics of the past, and Howard Beale (Peter Finch), the veteran TV newsman in *Network* (1976) whose desperate call for his viewers to "go to your nearest window and yell as loud as you can, 'I'm mad as hell and I'm not going to take it anymore!'" confirms that a responsible politics had been replaced by rage, spectacle, and, ultimately, futility. In kidnapping Patty Hearst, providing the media with tapes and photos, feeding the poor from the back of trucks, and robbing the Hibernia Bank with Patty in tow, the SLA had engaged in the politics of spectacle. Interestingly, *Network*'s Diana Christensen (Faye Dunaway), a producer immersed in the spectacle, imagines building on what Beale has created with a new show about "urban guerrillas." Referring to the audience that Beale had marshaled with his cries for help, film critic Roger Ebert wrote, "We can believe in the movie's 'Ecumenical Liberation Army' because nothing along those lines will amaze us after Patty Hearst."[58]

A third concept of survival involved something more than muddling through, getting by, or staying alive. It moved survival away from victimization and toward, or even up against, the heroic. Bailey knew of this other meaning, for he mentioned in his closing a powerful example of it—the incredible experience of survivors of a plane crash in the Andes Mountains on October 13, 1972, detailed in the 1974 book *Alive*. When rescuers located the plane's fuselage ten weeks later, it became clear that the sixteen survivors had quickly run out of food and, after some soul-searching, had begun to eat the well-preserved bodies of the dead. Moreover, the plane had been found only because two young men, defying bitter cold and a rugged terrain, had finally decided to risk everything in a desperate effort to go for help. An account from the *Detroit Free Press*, quoted on the book's cover, drew what must have been a common conclusion, calling the episode a "testimonial to the durability and determination of young men who might have chosen to die and simply would not."[59]

This concept of the survivor had been explored by English professor Terrence Des Pres in several essays published in the early 1970s and in a widely read book, *The Survivor: An Anatomy of Life in the Death Camps*, which appeared in 1976 and was based on accounts of those who had experienced the death camps and lived to tell their stories. Although Des Pres's work treated a subject—the emotional state of mind of camp inmates—that had been the focus of Patty Hearst's defense, his work was described, briefly, only once during the trial, and then by Joel Fort, a *government* witness. In *The Survivor*, Des Pres took issue with Lifton, Elkins, Bettelheim, and others who presented slaves and concentration camp inmates as passive victims of systems of total control. But he also held heroism at arm's length, arguing that in the camp context, the heroism of "dramatic defiance," of "glory and grand gesture" was equivalent to suicide. Between the passive victim and the defiant hero, Des Pres offered a "hardminded," fearless survivor who engaged in sabotage, theft, smuggling, collective disobedience, and other acts of resistance; who gave and shared and otherwise confirmed the social nature of humanity; who refused to "consent to death in any form"; and who lived not merely to preserve the self but to bear witness to horrors experienced and observed.[60] To be sure, Des Pres did not deny that the camps had produced victims. He understood the crushing pressures that were brought to bear on the self in the "extreme" situation of the camps, and he acknowledged that many inmates lacked the strength of body or will necessary to insist on the value of life in circumstances where abject hopelessness could seem the appropriate response. Yet his focus was on those who refused to despair and refused to be "simply a victim," and who chose not only to live but to live "humanly," with "decency intact," to "keep a living soul in a living body." For Des Pres, the survivor's most important quality was "dignity," a word that for him signified an "inward resistance to determination by external forces" and suggested "a sense of innocence and worth, something felt to be inviolate, autonomous and untouchable, and which is most vigorous when most threatened." It is, Des Pres concludes, "one of the irreducible elements of selfhood."[61]

At one extreme, this sort of situation pushes the concept of survival to a breaking point, where the desire to survive faces eclipse by another desire, independent—or nearly so—of the goal of survival: to risk one's life. To be sure, there have always been those who crave life-endangering risk. Yet it seems likely that the decade after 1975 witnessed a significant shift in the security/risk continuum. The rise of a cultlike worship of heroism (discussed below) was part of that shift. But its best expression was the publication in the spring of 1977 of the first issue of *Quest/77*, a new magazine for risk-takers and perhaps an early salvo in the "extreme sports" movement that would sweep the country at the end of the century. The cover featured Mount Everest, and a "Prologue" explained the magazine's philosophy and purpose. "The prevalence of fear," it began, "is man's chief blight. A touch of fear makes man survive, but too much of it stifles talent, freedom, and love. As dread negates life, so courage nurtures it." This issue contained a special section on "Courage," including a list of fears and phobias, and an article on "The Hero Business," which praised the work of the Carnegie Hero Commission for identifying rescuers who "knowingly and actually risked [their lives]."[62]

Bailey might have chosen to shoehorn Patty's experience into some version of the Des Pres—*Quest/77* concept of survival; indeed, his mention of the Andes plane crash was a gesture in that direction, a brief acknowledgment, perhaps, that the defense had erred in making Patty too much a victim, too little a survivor in the heroic, or near-heroic, mold. Bailey might, at that juncture, have presented Patty's decision to "join" the SLA as a decision akin to the Andes survivors' eating of human flesh, or argued that her participation in the Hibernia robbery was a high-risk act of courage, no different from striking out into a high-peaks wilderness. But Bailey could claim the qualities of Des Pres's fearless, righteous, life-affirming, resistant survivor for Patty only if she admitted to having fully and freely taken on that role as a member of the SLA. If, as the defense had repeatedly claimed, Patty had been brainwashed, coercively persuaded, or threatened into passivity, there wasn't much "dignity" to be found in her encounter with the SLA. Instead, Bailey's version of Patty Hearst was that of a kidnapped, abused, victimized woman consumed by the fear of dying, and doing everything she could to prevent it—everything, that is, except engaging in the one dramatic act that could have freed her. For Patty, survival consisted of hunkering down, living to see another day. Indeed, she was hunkered down even in the security of the federal courthouse, even as the trial began. "My biggest worry right now," she had confided in Bailey, "is staying alive."[63]

Stockholm Syndrome

Patty's sins of commission—taping those messages, attacking her family, joining the SLA, becoming a radical feminist, holding onto the monkey charm, even robbing the bank—could be explained, and might have been better understood, or even forgiven, had the jury and the American people been offered a convincing context for her behavior. Perhaps the *most* convincing context had been revealed just months before her abduction. In August 1973, four employees of the Sveriges Kreditbank in Stockholm, Sweden, were taken hostage by robbers, and after 131 hours a standoff with police ended without loss of life. In an exhaustive account of the event, published in the *New Yorker* in November 1974, during Patty's "missing year," Daniel Lang described how Kristin Ehnmark, a twenty-three-year-old hostage, had come to identify with her captors, allowing one of them to touch her breasts and hips and later insisting that the robbers had been "very nice." Most remarkably, after the crisis was over, she and the other hostages "persisted in thinking of the police as 'the enemy,' preferring to believe that it was the criminals to whom they owed their lives." Indeed, one of the hostages initiated a defense fund, and Ehnmark reportedly became engaged to one of her captors. Dr. Lennart Ljungberg, a clinical psychiatrist interviewed by Lang who had cared for the victims in the ten days following their rescue, referred to the conduct of the bank hostages as "identification with the aggressor," a term used by Dr. Anna Freud, adding that the phenomenon was known to have occurred at Auschwitz and among prisoners of war in Korea and Vietnam.[64]

Although the term "Stockholm syndrome," as a name for these and related phenomena, was apparently coined at the time of the bank robbery, it was not used by the American mass media until December 1979, when *Time* magazine suggested that the syndrome might have taken hold among those being held hostage by Iranian militants in Teheran. Not much in the way of scholarship appeared until after 1980, in response to mounting interest in the impact of hostage terrorism on the state of mind of captives. In *Victims of Terrorism* (1982), several scholars, most with backgrounds in psychiatry, explicitly applied the term to the Patty Hearst kidnapping, or described the phenomenon in ways that reflected her experience. One argued that under conditions of overwhelming fear and anxiety, a victim might "actively view the family and the police as the enemy"—as Patty, at one time or another, apparently distrusted her parents and the FBI. Another suggested that Patty's participation in the SLA's violent activities may have been a form of "identification with the captor" produced by a prolonged period of stress. David A. Soskis and Frank M. Ochberg focused on what they called the "positive half of the Stockholm Syndrome," the half that involved "affection for the captors," arguing that Patty's "feelings of affection" for her kidnappers and her "romantic and familial" comments about them, were neither unique nor remarkable, having been found in about half of "recent terrorist hostage cases." More recently, the term has been applied to the case of Elizabeth Smart, a fourteen-year-old kidnap victim who in 2002–2003 spent several months with her captors, even though unrestrained, after having been repeatedly raped and otherwise abused.[65]

Although the Stockholm syndrome does seem to describe the conduct of Smart and Hearst and has often been invoked with respect to their experiences, it may be a poor fit: in both cases, the victims claimed to have disliked their captors and to have cooperated only out of fear for their lives, suggesting a level of consciousness not present in accounts of the Stockholm event. By the same token, it seems likely that Bailey would have rejected a defense based on the Stockholm syndrome—had it been available at the time—because such a defense would have required the assumption that Patty was, if only in a confused way resulting from coercion and fear, deeply sympathetic to the SLA. From another perspective, however, the emergence of the syndrome as an explanation for certain kinds of conduct implies a fragile, vulnerable, malleable self that could be remade to carry out acts ostensibly inconsistent with the "real" self.

Patty's sin of omission was no less serious than those she had committed: she had not tried to escape. This too, she thought, could be explained, and without recourse to the idea that she had formed a bond of some kind with the SLA. She had been afraid, desperately afraid. First of Cinque, then of Saxbe and his FBI, then and always of Bill and Emily Harris, wherever they might be, of the Harris's contacts, whoever they were, of SLA members who had not yet been captured. Even in prison, and even while on trial. In a word, paranoid.

Paranoid

Patty's anxieties can be made to sound absurd, but they were not without foundation. Cinque was a megalomaniac. The Harrises were nasty, and Bill was a macho hothead with a gun. The Foster killing had bared the bloodthirsty side of the SLA. Only by chance had Patty escaped the Los Angeles shootout and fire. And in February 1976, after the trial had begun, San Simeon, the Hearst estate that had been one of Patty's childhood playgrounds, was bombed—a fact of which the jury was aware. Moreover, Patty's arguably irrational fears that the remnants of the SLA could reach her and kill her, even after her capture put her in police custody, were consistent with fears FBI special agent Thomas Strentz found among the hostage survivors of a 1976 Croatian skyjacking. Those victims, Strentz discovered, had dreams or nightmares that "expressed the fear," similar to Patty's, "that the subjects would escape from custody and recapture them."[66]

In addition, Patty's belief that the government was a shadowy and alien entity, not to be trusted, was hardly remarkable in an era that had experienced the Watergate break-in and cover-up, the burglary of the office of antiwar activist Daniel Ellsberg's psychiatrist, the revelations of the Senate's Church Committee that the CIA had plotted to assassinate the heads of foreign governments, including Patrice Lumumba (Congo) and Fidel Castro

(Cuba), the assassination of Black Panther leader Fred Hampton in a Chicago apartment by police acting on information provided by an FBI informant, and the news that the administration, headed by the prince of paranoia, Richard Nixon, was keeping an "enemies list" with hundreds of names—targets, as John Dean put it, of the administration's efforts to "use the available federal machinery to screw our political enemies."[67] One of the most horrific events of the decade, the November 1978 mass suicide-murder of 914 residents of the Peoples Temple project in Jonestown, Guyana, was triggered by leader Jim Jones's fear that his movement was the target of a CIA-orchestrated government conspiracy. Patty's fear of being killed by the FBI, confirmed for her by the LA shootout and fire, was not inconsistent with what she must have known about the conduct of law enforcement officers in recent prison breaks and uprisings, where the emphasis was usually on apprehending escapees or reasserting control, even if it meant endangering the lives of hostages. The most famous example was the police killing of ten hostages at the Attica Correctional Facility in New York State in 1971.[68]

Patty's sense that the SLA remained "out there," observing her conduct and capable of finding and punishing her at any time, was consistent with the recent experience of much of the New Left, which had been watched, infiltrated, and harassed by Nixon's FBI. Her anxieties were also consistent with the mid-1970s culture of surveillance, represented in Francis Ford Coppola's *The Conversation* (1974), perhaps the first film to have as its protagonist an expert in the secret observation of others. In the 1970s, writes cultural historian Stephen Paul Miller, "surveillance enters the lives of everyday characters." Nor was the "law" to be trusted to protect the innocent and punish the guilty. As a spate of Hollywood films—*Dirty Harry* (1971), *The French Connection* (1971), *Deliverance* (1972), *The Godfather* (1972), and *Serpico* (1973)—suggest, that function had been appropriated by or delegated to individuals or extralegal organizations.

To call the police might be dangerous. Patty would have to take care of herself.[69]

As cultural critic Timothy Melley has argued, participation in a culture of conspiracy offers the fragile self not just the anxiety (and pleasure) of having discovered and labeled one's enemies, but a curious form of identity, in which the individual is strengthened and fortified by imagining the self to be in imminent and perpetual danger.[70] I am conspired against, therefore I am. In that sense, Patty was an ideal vessel for conspiracy theories and other insights of the paranoid. She had struggled with the disjuncture between being a Hearst, which seemed to require an oversize personality and some knowledge of the history of one of America's most influential families, and being an ordinary, even uninteresting young woman, living in a shallow present, ungrounded. "People would ask me," she wrote in a note to Shana Alexander during the trial, "about H. castle [San Simeon] instead of talking to me like a *person*." Perhaps she suffered from the aimlessness of those who have so much money that they seldom face the need to do the things necessary to carve out an authentic self. [71]

But while Patty may have been more personally vulnerable to paranoid readings than some other Americans, she was hardly alone. Paranoia is a way of understanding, of making meaning, and it thrived in an era when traditional authorities—the police, teachers, parents, the clergy, politicians, corporate leaders, the military, presidents—had been found inadequate, harmful, old-fashioned, or dangerous. To the paranoid sensibility, the dramatic rise in gasoline prices that followed the Arab oil embargo in 1973 was plotted by the big oil companies; the globalization of the world economy was orchestrated by the Trilateral Commission, founded in 1973; the Kennedy assassination—for Nancy Ling Perry, a military coup designed to bring dictator Richard Nixon to power—was anything but the solitary act of Lee Harvey Oswald; and any light in the sky was a UFO.[72]

Afraid and paranoid. To understand Patty in those terms was reasonable, indeed, consistent with the survival culture of the day. Even so, staying alive was not enough. It was not enough for Alexander, who despaired at having reached the will-less core of Patty Hearst. It was not enough for the government's David Bancroft, who after the trial shared with Alexander his belief that Patty had used victimhood to mask the most exhilarating experience of her life, something "very vibrant, very real," a moment of genuine "buccaneering." As a consequence, Bancroft speculated, Patty would live her life as a lie or fantasy, unable to deal honestly with the choices she had made. "She was entitled to her guilt," Bancroft lamented. "Even little children have that. But she's been *evaporated*. Accountability is the name of the game, and they took her accountability away." And staying alive was not enough for the jurors, who preferred to believe Patty had lied than to accept the colorless, will-less victim the defense had presented, the "zombie" they saw every day in the courtroom. Sensing the jurors' intransigence on this point, Bailey had confronted them with the logic of their position. "Was it her duty to die," he asked, "to avoid committing a felony?"[73]

The Emerging Conservative Consensus

What had been required of Patty could not be articulated, at least not precisely. But it was clear that Patty had not done enough. In the broadest sense, she had failed to represent and articulate the emerging conservative political, social, and cultural consensus—the consensus that would elect Ronald Reagan, defeat the Equal Rights Amendment, begin the assault on feminism, attempt to ban abortion, challenge affirmative action, eliminate welfare, contest the forced busing of school children, revise ideas of crime and criminal justice, and make Sylvester Stallone and Arnold Schwarzenegger media idols—all, or most of it, in the name of what would soon be known as "family values." The emerging consensus would be represented by bodies, most of them "hard bodies"—Reagan on horseback, Rocky and Robocop and the Terminator, and *Iron John* (1990), Robert Bly's ode to masculinity. Patty's frail, stick-figure courtroom body, like Jimmy Carter's soft fireside persona and the "malaise" it represented, was on the way out. And Patty's legal case—cerebral and complex, dependent on experts and psychiatrists—spoke not to the body but to the mind.[74]

To be sure, the new consensus was not yet dominant. Patty's ordeal took place during a period of transition, when the postwar liberal consensus seemed still to prevail. Carter won the 1976 presidential election, defeating Gerald Ford; Reagan, whose strength was in the south and west, lacked a national following. The Equal Rights Amendment passed the Senate in 1972 and by 1977, championed by a powerful feminist movement, seemed headed for ratification, though the rate of state approvals had slowed markedly. Court-ordered busing to achieve racial integration had been violently opposed in Boston between 1974 and 1977, but even in the early 1980s it was by no means a defeated and rejected policy. Stallone made *Rocky* in 1976, but Schwarzenegger spent the seventies in a series of B movies, his appeal largely unrecognized. Soaring rates of divorce and cohabitation and the emergence of open gay relationships led many to lament the decline of the traditional nuclear family, but "family values" had not yet surfaced as a slogan identified primarily with the political and religious right.[75]

In the vanguard of the emerging consensus was the "silent majority," Richard Nixon's label for the resentful working- and lower-class whites who in the elections of 1968 and 1972 abandoned the Democratic Party and voted Republican. Their pied piper was Nixon's vice president, Spiro Agnew, who played to their sense of themselves as forgotten and abandoned Americans whose concerns had been ignored as liberal politicians catered to the whims of blacks, feminists, the poor, welfare recipients, elites, students, antiwar protesters, the counterculture, and East Coast intellectuals. They called for "law and order," which meant opposition to demonstrations and riots, rejection of measures favoring criminals' and prisoners' rights, retribution rather than rehabilitation as a goal of incarceration, and capital punishment, advocated by Nixon in his 1973 State of the Union address and reinstated by the United States Supreme Court in 1976 after a four-year suspension.[76]

For the "silent majority," Patty was the perfect object of disaffection and a powerful representation of what had gone wrong with America. As a Hearst, she was the quintessential symbol of privilege and wealth, made even more unappealing for having squandered her heritage in hippie Berkeley with pot-smoking Steven Weed. Kidnapped, she had shamefully assaulted her family with the new incivility of the young, mocking her parents and calling them "pigs."[77] By joining the SLA, she had weighed in with the undeserving enemies and competitors of the white, working-class male: blacks, feminists, criminals, the poor. And on trial, she had produced a defense that reeked of elitism (all those psychiatrists, all those experts) and threatened to extend permissiveness into new areas, further undermining the rule of law—and order. Of course, jurors did not admit to having been influenced by such considerations, nor could they. But the views of the silent majority undoubtedly helped shape the climate of opinion—public opinion and editorial opinion—within which the Hearst case was tried. When Bailey, speaking to the jury for the last time, insisted that he was not a "flaming liberal," he revealed a great concern: that he might be arguing his case to the silent majority.

Another "majority," the Moral Majority, organized by the Reverend Jerry Falwell, was not founded until 1979, the year Patty left jail, nor did the new religious right—a network of evangelical conservatives—come together until the late 1970s. But the larger movement of evangelicals and fundamentalists had been active and growing throughout the decade, galvanized by the nationwide legalization of abortion in *Roe v. Wade* (1973), the spectacle of national corruption that was Watergate, aggressive movements for women's and homosexual rights, "obscene" textbooks in West Virginia, and disgust with the purported decadence and immorality of the "sixties." For this group, Patty was anathema, a toxic symbol of permissiveness ("one of the movement's most often used words"), of feminism's challenge to patriarchy, of the decline of the family, and of a heterogeneity that threatened to upset the comfortable world of white America.[78]

Less obvious, perhaps, were the ways in which the Patty Hearst episode cut against the deep desire of the emerging Moral Majority for a clear, uncomplicated moral order. "The distinctive quality of evangelical popular religion," writes historian Erling Jorstad, "is its openness to believing that the great, complex questions of life can be answered clearly and directly." This craving for simplicity was frustrated by the maddening murkiness of Patty's case—and by what was perceived as her lack of the basic principles and values necessary to a grounded, moral life. Patty's ethics, asserted newspapers in Richmond, Virginia, and Winston-Salem, North Carolina, were those of situation and opportunity, akin to the relativistic "secular humanism" that was the avowed enemy of the religious right.[79]

The questions raised by Patty Hearst's saga were, indeed, of the "great, complex" sort: What was the essence of a human being? What could people be made to do? Was it possible to know the "real" Patty Hearst or, indeed, the "real" anyone? And the answers presented were not only complex but multiple and conflicting. Much of the trial was given over to evaluating Patty's conduct using abstruse analogies to wars, disasters, and the Holocaust; through it all, Patty's "essence" remained elusive. There was no clarity to be had, at least not easily. Against this ambiguity, consider Professor Walter Capps's summation of a sermon Falwell delivered in Lynchburg, Virginia, reveling in the moral clarity of the age of the apostles, when persecution had produced decisiveness: "It was either Yes or No, True or False, Right or Wrong, Good or Evil, Committed or Uncommitted. Either the Bible is the Word of God, or the Bible is not the Word of God. Either Jesus Christ is the only savior of humankind, or he is not."[80] Similarly, for the jury, either Patricia Hearst was a victim, or she had freely chosen a life of crime.

Falwell's black-and-white, either/or perspective would find its way into politics, dominating the presidency of George W. Bush, who through two terms seemed never to change his mind or to rethink a position, even on the presence in Iraq of weapons of mass destruction. It surfaced among Democratic candidates for the presidency in October 2007, during one of several debates that preceded the Iowa caucuses. Senator Hillary Clinton was the frontrunner at the time, and the media joined her main challengers, Senator Barack Obama and former Senator John

Edwards, in suggesting that her positions, on the Iraq war and other issues, were inconsistent and contradictory—the mark of a flawed candidacy and candidate. The matter came to a head when Clinton was asked her views on a controversial proposal by New York governor Eliot Spitzer to issue driver's licenses to illegal aliens. At one point Clinton said the plan "made a lot of sense," at another that "I did not say that it should be done." As the *New York Times* summarized the moment, "she at first seemed to defend it, then suggested she was against it," then accused the debate moderator of playing a game of "gotcha." The following week, Edwards kept the ball rolling. "We only need one mode from our president," he said. "Tell-the-truth mode all the time."

A few days later, on *Saturday Night Live*, a skit set at a Halloween party featured a cast member portraying Clinton, costumed in a bridal gown. Obama, making a cameo appearance, came as himself, explaining to his opponent's stand-in: "You know, Hillary, I have nothing to hide. I enjoy being myself. I'm not going to change who I am just because it's Halloween."[81] It was all in good fun, but the issues were serious. After all, charges of "flip-flopping," and of not being the Vietnam War hero he claimed to be, had derailed the 2004 presidential candidacy of Senator John Kerry.

The assault on Hillary Clinton recalled the not uncommon accusation that Patty was an opportunist who moved all too easily from "victim to revolutionary and back to victim." Under the headline "The Two Faces of Patty Hearst," one newspaper had asked, "Which is real?"—as if there were two, and only two, of which one necessarily was real. Hints of the fragmented self, framed in 1975 by the quest for coherence, continue to cause consternation—all the more so after three decades of Falwellian efforts to banish ambivalence, incongruity, complexity, even thoughtful discussion, from the public sphere. It was Patty's fate to go on trial just as the Christian right was emerging as a social and political force.[82]

Heroes

Even so, Patty might have triumphed in the courtroom, or at least in the court of public opinion, had she tried to escape—that is, had she been a hero. It could be argued, of course, that Patty had been just that. There was a bit of Clyde's Bonnie in Tania the bank robber, a touch of Annie Oakley in the young woman using *two* guns to defend her comrades outside Mel's, even something of Robin Hood in the SLA's efforts to feed the poor. There was, too, something heroic in Patty's extraordinary transformation, from bored rich kid, hostage to Steven Weed, to armed political feminist.

This view, however, faced several obstacles. The most obvious was Bailey's defense, which presented Patty as a cowering victim, desperate to save her life, sometimes confused, maybe brainwashed, but never heroic. Only the government was willing to grant that Patty possessed the hero's essential quality—free will—although its description of Patty as a "rebel in search of a cause" remained well shy of the heroic ideal. Imagine Robin Hood stealing from the rich only because he was bored.

A second obstacle had to do with the way in which Americans have traditionally understood and valued the different ways people have dealt with captivity, whether they were women abducted by Indians, slaves, or captured Korean War pilots. "Our cultural tradition," writes Edward M. Griffin, "teaches us to celebrate the escapee and accuse the unescaped captive of weakness, cowardice, or, worse, collusion." According to D. H. Lawrence, American writers have taken as their central theme a "frenzy for getting away from control of any sort," a proposition that makes sense of much of American literature, from James Fennimore Cooper's *The Last of the Mohicans* (1826) to J. D. Salinger's *The Catcher in the Rye* (1951).[83]

By the 1970s, captivity in a variety of forms—real, fictional, imagined, intellectualized—saturated the American outlook. More often than not, the captors were in remote areas abroad: in the Cambodian sanctuaries across the Vietnam border that threatened to reduce the "world's most powerful nation" to a "pitiful, helpless giant," in the words of Richard Nixon's April 30, 1970, address; in Saudi Arabia, Algeria, and the other OPEC nations, which held Americans captive to imported oil; in the fictional Vietnam of *The Deer Hunter* (1978), where the Vietcong fashioned a gruesome captivity for American soldiers, holding them in underwater riverbank cages and taking them to the brink of insanity with games of Russian roulette; and in Iran, where on November 4, 1979, militants stormed the U.S. embassy and took hostage sixty-six Americans, holding them captive for more than a year.[84] At home, Bruce Springsteen revealed the confined anguish of working-class men, trapped in a routine of mindless work and desperate leisure ("Working all day in my daddy's garage / Driving all night chasing some mirage"), and in her 1979 hit "I Will Survive," Gloria Gaynor expressed the growing unease of many young women, their expectations buoyed by the rising tide of feminism, confined in lackluster relationships to inadequate, spiritless men ("I'm not that chained up little person / Still in love with you"). A version of the captivity narrative seeped into academia, as scholars explored the dimensions of power and wrote about systems of domination and "social control," resurrecting Antonio Gramsci's concept of hegemony, Guy DeBord's "society of the spectacle," and Jeremy Bentham's panopticon (an eighteenth-century mechanism of observation and surveillance), while extolling the work of Michel Foucault on dominance through the creation and manipulation of "docile bodies."[85]

As potent as these ideas of captivity were, they were usually accompanied, even in the 1970s, by an antithesis, as if it were wrong or weak to give in to, or acknowledge, power and its effects. For Nixon, the specter of the "pitiful, helpless giant" called for a test of "will and character" and required the "action" that he announced that evening: the invasion of Cambodia. Springsteen's working-class protagonists refuse to accept fully life's meager offerings ("Show a little faith, there's magic in the night"), and Gaynor finds the strength to send her man packing. Scholars of power either recognized and celebrated resistance or were soon overshadowed by those who did. As a system of domination, hegemony was found to require a degree of vigilance that left it vulnerable to challenges; even the ubiquitous spectacle could be challenged through techniques of intervention that DeBord himself had pioneered. By 1980 if not before, the victim was out, and agency was in.[86]

This didn't work for Patty. Her "frenzy," if indeed she experienced one, was not about getting away, not about being "masterless," as Lawrence had put it. Instead, it was about being "mastered," and that, writes Griffin, made Patty a "bad captive," and made her story—her captivity narrative—one that Americans were not eager to celebrate.[87]

A third obstacle to understanding Patty Hearst as a heroic figure was the nature of the heroic in the 1970s. At its center was widespread anguish over what one popular magazine labeled "The Vanishing American Hero," another "Disappearing Heroes," a third "The End of the American Hero." In 1977, when *Senior Scholastic* asked fifteen thousand students to name a living "personal hero," the fourth most common response—after Farrah Fawcett-Majors, Jerry Lewis, and Romanian gymnast Nadia Comaneci, was "no hero at all."[88] There were, to be sure, good reasons for this dire perspective on contemporary heroism; the Watergate scandal had tainted politicians, and a defeat in Vietnam had tarred the battlefield. But there was more to the decline-of-the-heroic critique than the reality of a gloomy present. Heroism had its own politics. Very often, the point of disparaging the current state of heroism was to identify the apparent absence of heroes with the liberal values and movements of the 1960s and early 1970s, and to encourage Americans to embrace a new, more conservative social ethic that privileged the white male and the militarized nation state—back to the fifties, in effect. This version of heroism appealed to, and was designed to attract, white, working-class men: Nixon's silent majority, later Reagan Democrats. Hence *The Last American Hero*, the title of a 1973 film docudrama, referred to Junior Johnson, a stock-car driver.

In the symbolic politics of heroism in the 1970s, the POW issue loomed large, taking on a magnitude out of all proportion to the number of men involved. For the Nixon administration, mired in a war in Vietnam that would end soon in humbling defeat, the obsession with POWs was ideological. As Andreas Killen argues, in 1973 Nixon used his frequent welcoming sessions for released POWS to establish an iconic image of the POW as triumphant male hero, a figure of resistance unchanged by years of captivity, doggedly clinging to his faith in American institutions. Even as the withdrawal of American troops signaled a humiliating end to the long war, the image of the immutable POW stood for a curious sort of victory, or at least a refusal to be defeated, and it foreshadowed a decade-long effort to use the POW issue to recast and redefine the conflict in Vietnam.[89] For our purposes, the prominence of the POW issue in national politics in the mid-1970s exposes the ideological currents that swirled through Patty's trial as the defense sought to associate Patty with victimized Korean War POWs and the prosecution tried just as hard to dismiss the analogy or, indeed, any relationship to the prisoners of any war. More was at stake than Patty's future. If the Patty/POW link was found to be valid, to explain her conduct, it would have reflected badly on the new, highly political image of the Vietnam POW, threatening to destabilize that image and to disrupt the campaign on which it was based. And it would have allowed a woman into the heroic pantheon.

Patty's big problem—her failure to escape, or even to *try* to escape—might profitably be understood in the context of two cinematic treatments of escape, one made about a decade before the kidnapping, the other about a decade after. Made at the hubristic height of the "American Century," *The Great Escape* (1963) features a clever and glorious mass escape from a World War II German prisoner of war camp, highlighted by "Cooler King" Hilts (Steve McQueen), astride a motorcycle, leaping a fence to freedom in Switzerland. Americans (and their Allies, too) could do anything they wanted to do. *Rambo: First Blood Part II* (1985) was made as American ambitions were being revived by Reagan after the debacle in Vietnam and the Carter "malaise"—exemplified for many by the taking of American hostages in Iran in 1979. This film also features an escape attempt, led by John Rambo (Sylvester Stallone), a heavily muscled new American male, who takes on the task of liberating the quintessential "victims": American POWs in Vietnam.[90] Although *Rambo II* fell short of claiming that the POWs could engineer and bring off their own escape, it did, like *The Great Escape*, suggest that escape was the only solution to captivity, and in Rambo, it offered a figure equivalent in stature to "Cooler King."

Patty's ordeal was framed, chronologically, by Steve McQueen and Sylvester Stallone, the former playing some version of the heroic American past, the latter what America—or some significant portion of it—wanted to become. During the 1970s, the great American anxiety was the anxiety of captivity—the captivity of cult followers, of those held hostage by Iranian militants, of the POWs, of Patty Hearst in the closet—each instance a reminder that U.S. power was in decline. It was understood that relief would come from right-minded men who took action.[91] There was no place in this framework for what Patty was or claimed to be. There was no place for a "woman with a gun," a figure that for many stood for radical feminism at its most dangerous; even Co Bao, Rambo's gun-carrying love interest in *First Blood*, must die, if only to allow the rejuvenated warrior male to complete the mission on his own, free from the corrupting effects of a woman's assistance. There was no place for Patty's new politics, deeply indebted not only to feminism but to the liberal/radical agenda identified with the 1960s: concern for blacks, prisoners, the poor, those on relief, third world peoples. In the realm of the hero, defined by the coherent individual engaged in an act of will, there was no room for the multiple, fragmented, confused, or cognitively impaired selves with which Patty had become identified during her captivity and trial. Even though the government raised the possibility in making its case, there was no room in the heroic model for the possibility that Patty had learned something about power and patriarchy from her captors and might have used that knowledge to carve out a new, less traditional, female identity.[92] For the working-class silent majority, who were being encouraged to believe that "elites" were the real enemy[93] and somehow responsible for the decline of American industry, there was no way to reconcile Patty's heritage as a Hearst, her family's wealth, with prevailing ideas of heroism. Most important, there was no place for what Patty had told the jury and the American people she was: a fragile, paranoid, frightened young woman, desperate to survive. In 1974, the Hearst family cook had brazenly suggested that Patty might have been better off dead, consumed with the rest of the SLA in the Los Angeles fire, for at least then she would have been a hero, in the Joan of Arc mold.[94] When, in closing, Bailey turned to the jury and asked, "was it her duty to die, to avoid committing a felony?" it seems likely that more than one juror—and perhaps a majority of Americans—said to themselves, "Yes," or "Maybe."

At fifty-year intervals in the late nineteenth and twentieth centuries, great public trials, media spectacles all, captured the American imagination. In 1875 Henry Ward Beecher, the nation's best-known Protestant minister, and much-admired, went on trial in Brooklyn, New York, charged with having committed adultery with Elizabeth Tilton, a member of his parish and the wife of Theodore Tilton, a close friend. In the midsummer heat of Dayton, Tennessee, in 1925, three-time Democratic presidential candidate William Jennings Bryan took center stage, defending a biblical view of creation while serving as prosecuting attorney in a case against John Scopes, a high school science teacher accused of teaching evolution in violation of a recently passed state law. The third trial, of course, was of Patty Hearst.

The Beecher-Tilton scandal and the Scopes trial achieved iconic status not because their protagonists were men of stature and fame or because observers were especially interested in the law that would be made in each case. These events riveted audiences because they placed in relief the central conflicts, tensions, and anxieties of the age, peeling the cultural onion to reveal layer upon layer of meaning. Taking place on the eve of an unprecedented industrial and urban revolution, the Beecher-Tilton scandal found many Americans aghast at the world they sensed lay just ahead and nostalgic for the one they were leaving behind. The episode allowed the past to be read as an era of piety, religion, civilization, Victorian privacy and concealment, the notion of "character," and an uncompromising Calvinism; the future was understood as worldly, secular, immoral, tainted with modern ideas about openness and exposure, the emerging concept of "personality" (though it wasn't called that yet), and a culture of sentimentalism. Although religion was again central to the Scopes trial, a half century of social and economic change had yielded a set of oppositions not limited to the religious: fundamentalism versus modernism, and faith versus science, but also country versus city, age versus youth, the common folk versus educated experts, and a conservative South versus a liberal, cosmopolitan North and East.[95]

Trials are essentially contests between adversaries, better suited to sharpening differences than to reconciling them.

Reconciliation is the province of the hero. Not two years after Scopes's conviction, Charles Lindbergh's epic solo flight across the Atlantic again placed in bold relief some of the same dichotomies: age/youth, rural/urban, faith/science. But it also brought together two elements that had theretofore seemed antithetical, celebrating the historic flight as the triumph of *both* the self-sufficient individual (the "lone eagle") and the machine (the *Spirit of St. Louis*) and thus gave Americans the opportunity to deal with a primal cultural anxiety.[96]

That sort of magic was surely beyond Patty, whose heroism, had she been up to it, would have been limited to escaping, a dramatic act (depending on the circumstances) but not the sort of freely chosen, death-defying adventure Lindbergh had achieved. Patty could not reconcile psychiatry's emphasis on causation with the law's on individual responsibility; she could not define a middle ground between determinism and free will, or arbitrate the conflict between elite experts and a rising populist enthusiasm for so-called common sense; she could not calm the critics of "permissiveness" or modulate a growing working-class rage directed against feminism, rich people, college kids, and the counterculture; she could not bridge the gap between the 1960s' valorization of the victim and the 1980s' elevation of resistance, between the survivor and the hero. Having experienced life as Patty and Tania and Pearl and having resigned a life of inherited luxury for one of flight and squalid criminality, she could not calm the fears of those who wondered if the fragile, fractured self would ever again cohere.

No, she was not up to those tasks. Nor, in an age without heroes, was anyone else. Even so, Patty was there at every turn, every impasse. For a few years in the mid-1970s, her story was available for every debate, her adventure fodder for every conflict over ideas and values, every discussion about the nation's past and its future, every editor looking to make a point about college campuses, crime, terrorism, women with guns, the perils of wealth, or any of a dozen other hot topics. In the days and weeks after her abduction, Patty's story was at first distinct from that of the SLA, and she was predictably, and appropriately, understood as the victim of a brutal political kidnapping. Yet even then Patty's hold on the status of victim was tenuous, out of sync with an age obsessed with what had gone wrong, a culture that had come to see the concept of the victim as better suited to making excuses than to fixing responsibility and changing behavior.

After the Hibernia robbery, as her story merged with that of the SLA, Patty became a vehicle for the expression of a wide variety of cultural anxieties and critical perspectives. For many Americans, and especially those on the right, she came to represent the out-of-control, self-indulgent, permissive sixties; feminism run amok, armed and sexualized; the pathology of left-wing politics; the arrogance of a moneyed elite; the coddling of criminals. The trial, in a bicentennial year more desperate than celebratory, as the nation was grinding its way to the right, only deepened and broadened these concerns. The parade of psychiatrists to the stand, testifying to the power of coercive persuasion and raising the specter of brainwashing, heightened fears that every antisocial act would be explained, understood, even tolerated, with dire consequences for the battle against crime. As one defense witness after another interpreted Patty's conduct in the light of the experience of concentration camp inmates and prisoners of war in Korea and Vietnam, many Americans remained unconvinced or skeptical, while others recoiled at these reminders of the nation's inchoate sense of itself as limited, confined, and captive.

The government won not because Browning and Bancroft understood Patty better than Bailey and Johnson, and not because their version of events more accurately described what had happened. Patty went to jail because the government's story was the one Americans wanted to hear at that moment in the mid-1970s; they had had their fill of victims, wanted more than mere survival, and yearned to shed the yoke of determinism.

At its core, this was a story of agency, of Patricia Hearst, willful and independent, rejecting one life and choosing another. It was a story of rebellions large and small, against the day-to-day sexism of Steven Weed, against the restrictions of a Hearst identity, against nuns and parents, against wealth and the power of wealth. And it was a story of choices made: the choice to join the SLA, to participate in the Hibernia robbery, to fire away at Mel's, to tolerate Bill Harris's anger and violence, to learn feminism from Wendy Yoshimura, to stand on the side of social justice, and—most telling of all—not to try to escape. In the end, this story was less about Patty than about what Americans wanted to believe of themselves: that they were a resilient people, possessed of free will, capable of transcending the malaise that was settling over the nation, capable even, as Patricia Hearst had not been, of heroism.

notes

Introduction

1. *The Trial of Patty Hearst* (San Francisco: Great Fidelity Press, 1976), Hearst testimony, pp. 154 ("bitch"), 196. Patricia Campbell Hearst, with Alvin Moscow, *Every Secret Thing* (Garden City, NY: Doubleday, 1982), pp. 29–33.

2. The best essay-length summary of the Hearst case is Janice Schuetz, *The Logic of Women on Trial: Case Studies of Popular American Trials* (Carbondale: Southern Illinois University Press, 1994), pp. 161–83. See also Charles Patrick Ewing and Joseph T. McCann, *Minds on Trial: Great Cases in Law and Psychology* (New York: Oxford University Press, 2006), pp. 31–43.

3. Steven Weed, *My Search for Patty Hearst* (New York: Crown Publishers, 1976), pp. 3 ("routinized"), 9–10 (Venice); John Pascal and Andy Port, "An Idyllic Existence Turns to Nightmare," *Boston Globe*, 27 May 1974, p. 1; Vin McLellan and Paul Avery, *The Voices of Guns* (New York: G. P. Putnam's Sons, 1977), p. 230 ("two kids").

4. Hearst, *Every Secret Thing*, pp. 4, 9–10.

5. McLellan and Avery, *Voices of Guns*, p. 261. Excerpts from several of the SLA audiotapes and other documents are at http://faculty.uml.edu/sgallagher/patty_hearst.htm (accessed 29 February 2008).

6. Ibid., p. 332.

7. Shana Alexander, *Anyone's Daughter* (New York: Viking Press, 1979), p. 65.

8. Anthony Giddens, *Modernity and Self-Identity: Self and Society in the Late Modern Age* (Stanford, CA: Stanford University Press, 1991); Irvin G. Wyllie, *The Self-Made Man in America* (New York: Free Press, 1966).

9. Sam Binkley, *Getting Loose: Lifestyle Consumption in the 1970s* (Durham, NC: Duke University Press, 2007), pp. 3, 6.

10. Alexander, *Anyone's Daughter*, pp. 145, 191, 399, 401.

11. Ibid., pp. 191, 234, 402, 521, 532.

The Story

1. Janice Schuetz, *The Logic of Women on Trial: Case Studies of Popular American Trials* (Carbondale: Southern Illinois University Press, 1994), pp. 162–63; Vin

McLellan and Paul Avery, *The Voices of Guns* (New York: G. P. Putnam's Sons, 1977), pp. 58–67, 58n.

2. Shana Alexander, *Anyone's Daughter* (New York: Viking Press, 1979), pp. 136–37, 143–44; McLellan and Avery, *Voices of Guns*, pp. 51–52 (political prisoners), 68–69 ("Black Judas"), 138–42, 111 (DeFreeze decision), 132–36 (memorandum).

3. McLellan and Avery, *Voices of Guns*, pp. 132 (Panthers), 144 (Dohrn).

4. McLellan and Avery, *Voices of Guns*, pp. 35 (credit check), 112–13, 78; "Willie—'Very Easily Led,'" *Montgomery* (AL) *Advertiser*, 19 May 1974, p. 5E; Martin Arnold, "Harrises Internal Revolution," *Sacramento Bee*, 19 September 1975, pp. A18–19; "Friends: Road to Radicalism," *Montgomery Advertiser*, 19 September 1975, p. 33.

5. "FBI Charges Patricia in Shootout at Store," *Montgomery Advertiser*, 20 May 1974, pp. 1–2; Albert Parry, *Terrorism: From Robespierre to Arafat* (New York: Vanguard Press, 1976), p. 348; "SLA's 'Mizmoon' Was Conforming Honors Student in High School," *Montgomery Advertiser*, 19 May 1974, p. 5E; "SLA's Ms. Perry: From Topless to Revolutionary?" *Montgomery Advertiser*, 19 May 1974, p. 11D; McLellan and Avery, *Voices of Guns*, pp. 116 (Hall), 117 (Soltysik), 175–77 (Perry).

6. Alexander, *Anyone's Daughter*, pp. 150–51; Parry, *Terrorism*, p. 347; McLellan and Avery, *Voices of Guns*, p. 81.

7. McLellan and Avery, *Voices of Guns*, pp. 121, 112.

8. Alexander, *Anyone's Daughter*, p. 136; "The Symbionese Liberation Army," http://www.black-dahlia.org/sla-print.html (accessed 12 February 2008); Parry, *Terrorism*, pp. 344–45; McLellan and Avery, *Voices of Guns*, pp. 317–18.

9. Editorial, *Charlotte* (NC) *Observer*, 27 May 1974, reprinted in *Editorials on File*, vol. 5 (New York: Facts on File, 1974), p. 632 ("vision"); editorial, *Richmond News Leader*, 21 May 1974, *Editorials on File*, 5:629 ("cause").

10. Patricia Campbell Hearst, with Alvin Moscow, *Every Secret Thing* (Garden City, NY: Doubleday, 1982), p. 69 ("Fascist Insect"); *The Symbionese Liberation Army: Documents and Communications*, ed. Robert Brainard Pearsall (Amsterdam: Rodopi. N. V., 1974), p. 37 (public schools); McLellan and Avery, *Voices of Guns*, pp. 75–76 (Harris letter), 277 (feminism).

11. Parry, *Terrorism*, pp. 344 (Peking House), 347, 346 ("fascist capitalist class"); Hearst, *Every Secret Thing*, pp. 72 (SLA reading), 71 (violence). On the SLA's Maoism, see McLellan and Avery, *Voices of Guns*, pp. 58, 59n, 263.

12. *The Trial of Patty Hearst* (San Francisco: Great Fidelity Press, 1976), Hearst testimony, pp. 61, 154–55; hereafter referred to as *Trial Transcript*. McLellan and Avery, *Voices of Guns*, pp. 18 (Cinque Mtume), 281 (blindfolded). The conditions under which Patty was held were the subject of debate at her trial. McLellan and Avery make the good point that even the "Tania Interview," composed by Patty and the Harrises months later, and written for publication, paints the experience as disorienting, physically uncomfortable, and oppressive (p. 281).

13. Hearst, *Every Secret Thing*, pp. 44 ("Codes of War"), 49–51 ("interrogation"), 63, 69 (food program), 59 (sexual assault); *Trial Transcript* (Hearst testimony), p. 158 (sexual assault). For the contents of the tape, see McLellan and Avery, *Voices of Guns*, pp. 204–5, 208.

14. Hearst, *Every Secret Thing*, p. 72 ("nonsense," "sheltered"); *Trial Transcript*, p. 161.

15. Hearst, *Every Secret Thing*, p. 79 ("one day at a time"); Alexander, *Anyone's Daughter*, p. 377 (Fort).

16. Hearst, *Every Secret Thing*, pp. 83–86.

17. Ibid., pp. 90 ("join us"), 93–94 (sex); *Trial Transcript* (Hearst testimony), p. 165; McLellan and Avery, *Voices of Guns*, p. 217 (document by SLA women). Although Patty wrote in her book that sex with Cinque took place the day after Wolfe's visit, she testified that the encounter took place a week later. The account offered here of Patty's sexual contacts with the SLA seems the most plausible. However, drafts of the "Tania Interview" suggest the possibility that Patty had experienced a genuine political conversion before these sexual encounters, and that she chose to sleep with Cujo and, less likely, Cinque. See McLellan and Avery, *Voices of Guns*, pp. 287–88.

18. Hearst, *Every Secret Thing*, pp. 99–101; Alexander, *Anyone's Daughter*, p. 427 (Kozol). Edward M. Griffin compares Patty Hearst's decision to join her captors with that of Mary Jemison, a fifteen-year-old white woman captured in 1758 by Shawnee Indians and French soldiers and later purchased by the Senecas. Jemison chose to establish a new life with those who held her captive. Edward M. Griffin, "Patricia Hearst and Her Foremothers: The Captivity Fable in America," *Centennial Review* 36 (Spring 1992): 311–26, esp. 314–15.

19. Editorial, *Arizona Republic*, 5 April 1974, *Editorials on File*, 5:443; "Patricia Renounces Her Family," *Montgomery Advertiser*, 4 April 1974, p. 1 (Randolph and Catherine Hearst quotations); McLellan and Avery, *Voices of Guns*, pp. 225 (Catherine Hearst), 226 ("disgrace"); John A. Lester, *Girl in a Box: The Untold Story of the Patricia Hearst Kidnap* (San Jose, CA: Shoestring Publications, 2004), pp. 48, 68, 73, 87, 49, 117–18

20. McLellan and Avery, *Voices of Guns*, p. 368 (tape); Lester, *Girl in a Box*, p. 223 ("shot in the car"); editorial, "A Strange Case," *Montgomery Advertiser*, 5 April 1974, p. 4; editorial, *Chicago American* ("Today" section), 8 April 1974, *Editorials on File*, 5:443.

21. "Patricia Renounces Her Family," *Montgomery Advertiser*, 4 April 1974, p. 1 (authorities undecided); "Kidnap-Victim Patricia Charged with Kidnapping," *Montgomery Advertiser*, 23 May 1974, pp. 1–2. See also Griffin, "Patricia Hearst and Her Foremothers," p. 320.

22. Hearst, *Every Secret Thing*, pp. 102 (not brainwashed), 102–10 (photographed), 112 (issued gun), 118 (Tania), 116 (toothbrush), 121 (monkey); Alexander, *Anyone's Daughter*, p. 180 (tape).

23. Hearst, *Every Secret Thing*, p. 154; *Trial Transcript* (Hearst testimony), p. 174; McLellan and Avery, *Voices of Guns*, p. 274 (sign).

24. Hearst, *Every Secret Thing*, pp. 175, 204, 211, 210 ("prophet"), 213; Alexander, *Anyone's Daughter*, p. 195; *Trial Transcript* (Hearst testimony), p. 177.

25. Hearst, *Every Secret Thing*, p. 215 ("trained and drilled"); *Trial Transcript* (Hearst testimony), p. 178.

26. *Trial Transcript* (Hearst testimony), p. 230; Hearst, *Every Secret Thing*, pp. 216 (Pavlov, "soldier"), 215 ("what the fuck").

27. Parry, *Terrorism*, p. 360; *Trial Transcript* (Matthews testimony), pp. 84–86.

28. Hearst, *Every Secret Thing*, pp. 232–37.Randolph and Catherine Hearst also saw these events unfold on television. For their reaction, and a media account of the incident, see Lester, *Girl in a Box*, pp. 155–72.

29. Editorial, (Little Rock) *Arkansas Democrat*, 24 April 1974, *Editorials on File*, 5:447 (Kent State); editorial, *Akron Beacon Journal*, 16 February 1974, *Editorials on File*, 5:195; editorial, *Springfield* (MA) *Union*, 20 February 1974, *Editorials on File*, 5:196; editorial, *Atlanta Constitution*, 16 February 1974, *Editorials on File*, 5:195.

30. *Editorials on File*, narrative of events, 5:439 ("common criminals"); editorial, *Washington Post*, 21 April 1974, *Editorials on File*, 5:446; editorial, *Arkansas Democrat*, 23 April 1974, *Editorials on File*, 5:447; editorial, *Cleveland Press*, 20 April 1974, *Editorials on File*, 5:445; editorial, (Toledo) *Blade*, 20 April 1974, *Editorials on File*, 5:445.

31. Hearst, *Every Secret Thing*, pp. 246, 379.

32. Editorial, *Washington Star News*, 3 March 1974, *Editorials on File*, 5:440; editorial, *Arizona Republic*, 5 April 1974, *Editorials on File*, 5:443.

33. Jay Cantor, *The Space Between: Literature and Politics* (Baltimore: Johns Hopkins University Press, 1981), p. 78. The book contains a chapter on Patty Hearst.

34. Editorial, *Emporia* (KS) *Gazette*, 25 May 1974, *Editorials on File*, 5:631; editorial, (Oklahoma City) *Daily Oklahoman*, 9 February 1974, *Editorials on File*, 5:191 ("down our noses"); "Patty's Release May be Imminent," *Montgomery Advertiser*, 3 April 1974, p. 2 (Saxbe claim).

35. "The SLA: A Frightening Precedent for U.S. Terror?" *Chicago Sun-Times*, 28 May 1974, p. 44 (Rapoport, with *Los Angeles Times* byline); editorial, (Portland) *Oregonian*, 20 September 1975, *Editorials on File*, 6:1140; editorial, *Arkansas Democrat*, 26 February 1974, *Editorials on File*, 5:198; editorial, *Daily Oklahoman*, 9 February 1974, *Editorials on File*, 5:191.

36. McLellan and Avery, *Voices of Guns*, pp. 250 (hams), 242–43, 247.

37. Editorial, (Baltimore) *AfroAmerican*, 19 February 1974, *Editorials on File*, 5:191; editorial, *Indianapolis Star*, 14 February 1974, *Editorials on File*, 5:192; editorial, *Indianapolis Star*, 17 March 1974, *Editorials on File*, 5:441; McLellan and Avery, *Voices of Guns*, p. 251 (Reagan).

38. Editorial, *Emporia Gazette*, 19 February 1974, *Editorials on File*, 5:194; editorial, *Buffalo Evening News*, 15 February 1974, *Editorials on File*, 5:194; editorial, *Hartford Courant*, 1 March 1974, *Editorials on File*, 5:440; editorial, *Dayton Daily News*, 14 February 1974, *Editorials on File*, 5:193; editorial, *Wichita Eagle*, 14 February 1974, *Editorials on File*, 5:195.

39. Editorial, *Wall Street Journal*, 14 February 1974, *Editorials on File*, 5:193.

40. Philip Jenkins, *Decade of Nightmares: The End of the Sixties and the Making of Eighties America* (New York: Oxford University Press, 2006), p. 5.

41. Editorial, *Dallas Morning News*, 9 February 1974, *Editorials on File*, 5:191; editorial, *Birmingham* (AL) *News*, 25 February 1974, *Editorials on File*, 5:196; editorial, *Charlotte Observer*, 27 May 1974, *Editorials on File*, 5:632. For a summary of the Murphy kidnapping, see the February 20 1974 entry at http://www.safran-arts.com/42day/history/h4feb/h4feb20.html#kidnap (accessed 22 February 2008).

42. Alexander, *Anyone's Daughter*, pp. 180–81 (5th tape), 44, 127 (6th tape).

43. Editorial, *Winston-Salem* (NC) *Journal*, 5 April 1974, *Editorials on File*, 5:442 ("irrelevant rag," Weed); editorial, *San Francisco Sun-Reporter*, 20 April 1974, *Editorials on File*, 5:444. Bob Greene, "Is She Just a Crazy Little Girl?" *Chicago Sun-*

Times, 21 September 1975, p. 6; editorial, *Dayton Daily News*, 21 September 1975, *Editorials on File*, 6:1141.

44. Quoted in Alexander, *Anyone's Daughter*, p. 428.

45. William Graebner, "Dr. Benjamin Spock," in *Leaders from the 1960s: A Biographical Sourcebook of American Activism*, ed. David DeLeon (Westport, CT: Greenwood Press, 1994), p. 228.

46. Jenkins, *Decade of Nightmares*, pp. 6, 126–27, 119.

47. Editorial, *Manchester Union Leader*, 14 May 1974, *Editorials on File*, 5:628; editorial, *Roanoke* (VA) *Times*, 2 March 1974, *Editorials on File*, 5:439; editorial, *St. Louis Globe-Democrat*, 6 March 1974, *Editorials on File*, 5:441; McLellan and Avery, *Voices of Guns*, p. 252 (death penalty reinstatement).

48. Editorial, *Richmond News Leader*, 21 May 1974, *Editorials on File*, 5:629; Jeremiah V. Murphy, "There Are Signs That Permissiveness for Youth Is Not the Magic Answer," *Boston Globe*, 23 September 1975, p. 23.

49. Hearst, *Every Secret Thing*, pp. 22 ("no radicals"), 23, 5 ("not spoiled"), 6–7; Steven Weed, *My Search for Patty Hearst* (New York: Crown Publishers, 1976), pp. 3, 5, 9, 20.

50. Mike Royko, "If Patty Isn't Guilty, Why'd She Do It?" *Los Angeles Times*, 25 March 1976, sect. 2, p. 7 ("spoiled rich kid"); "On Angels, Pot and Patty," (New Orleans) *Times-Picayune*, 27 September 1975, p. 14 ("wayward child"); Malcolm B. Johnson, "Patty's Conviction Fit Nation's Need, Mood," *Miami Herald*, 25 March 1976, p. 7A ("rebellious miscreant"); editorial, "Patty, Squeaky & Co.," *Times-Picayune*, 20 September 1975, sect. 1, p. 12 ("naughty children").

51. Editorial, *Indianapolis News*, 25 September 1975, *Editorials on File*, 6:1093.

52. Hearst, *Every Secret Thing*, pp. 243–44.

53. Krin Gabbard and Glenn O. Gabbard, *Psychiatry and the Cinema* (Chicago: University of Chicago Press, 1987); Janet Walker, *Couching Resistance: Women, Film, and Psychoanalytic Psychiatry* (Minneapolis: University of Minnesota Press, 1993); *The Warren Report: Report of the President's Commission on the Assassination of President John F. Kennedy* (n.p.: Associated Press, n.d.), p. 160; U.S. Department of Labor, Office of Policy Planning and Research, *The Negro Family: The Case for National Action*, March 1965 (n.p., n.d.), pp. 6, 19, and the page preceding the table of contents.

54. Editorial, *Wall Street Journal*, 14 February 1974, *Editorials on File*, 5:193; editorial, *Kansas City Times*, 14 February 1974, *Editorials on File*, 5:194; editorial, *Richmond News Leader*, 21 May 1974, *Editorials on File*, 5:629; editorial, *Times-Picayune*, 25 May 1974, *Editorials on File*, 5:630 (Hitler, Manson family); editorial, *Salt Lake Tribune*, 22 May 1974, *Editorials on File*, 5:632 (alienated neuroticism).

55. Editorial, *Arizona Republic*, 27 May 1974, *Editorials on File*, 5:631 ("mad dog"); "SLA's Leader 'Cinque' Killed Self, Coroner Says," *Atlanta Journal*, 25 May 1974, p. 3-B. The *Dayton Daily News* used the phrase "mad dog extremists" (editorial, *Editorials on File*, 2 March 1974, 5:439).

56. "Patty, Squeaky & Co.," *Times-Picayune* ("crazies," "psychos"); editorial, *Kansas City Times*, 20 September 1975, *Editorials on File*, 6:1144 ("madness of alienation"); editorial, *Chicago Daily Defender*, 23 September 1975, *Editorials on File*, 6:1144 ("mentally sick people").

57. Victoria Graham, "Wealthy Fugitive," *Sacramento Bee*, 19 September 1975, p. A18; Greene, "Is She Just a Crazy Little Girl?"

58. Hearst, *Every Secret Thing*, pp. 282–83, 294, 287 (code names), 300 (Yoshimura); Alexander, *Anyone's Daughter*, p. 206; Richard Gid Powers, *Broken: The Troubled Past and Uncertain Future of the FBI* (New York: Free Press, 2004), p. 331 (Tubman).

59. Alexander, *Anyone's Daughter*, pp. 64–65, 75, 113, 94 ("street signs"), 65 ("freedom fighter," "photograph"), 91–92 ("anything I'm told"), 113, 328 ("Tania exists").

60. Hearst, *Every Secret Thing*, pp. 324, 344, 335 ("chain-smoked").

61. McLellan and Avery, *Voices of Guns*, p. 484.

62. Hearst, *Every Secret Thing*, pp. 375, 356, 365, 376 ("mental peace"); McLellan and Avery, *Voices of Guns*, pp. 492–94; "Ends Massive FBI Hearst Hunt," *New York Times* story printed in *Montgomery Advertiser*, 19 September 1975, p. 1 (Catherine Hearst).

63. "Judge Orders Patty Held without Bond," *Sacramento Bee*, 20 September 1975, p. 1 (weapons); Hearst, *Every Secret Thing*, p. 379.

64. "Ends Massive FBI Hearst Hunt," *Montgomery Advertiser* (braless, hips); Jack V. Fox, "The Two Faces of Patty Hearst," *Chicago Sun-Times*, 21 September 1975, p. 5 ("fist salute"). On the "urban guerrilla" remark, see Alexander, *Anyone's Daughter*, p. 209; "Judge Revokes Patty's Bail; Recites Risk," *Montgomery Advertiser*, 20 September 1975, p. 5 (two references to "urban guerrilla"); editorial, *Dayton Daily News*, 21 September 1975, *Editorials on File*, 6:1141.

65. *Trial Transcript* (Hearst testimony), p. 242; Alexander, *Anyone's Daughter*, p. 439; Hearst, *Every Secret Thing*, p. 387; "Patty Fears She'll Be 'Prisoner' of Parents," *Des Moines Register*, 26 September 1975, p. 1.

66. "Postscript: Famous Prisoner Shifted Course of Guard's Life," *Los Angeles Times*, 24 October 1977, sect. 2, p. 1 ("more about guns"); Hearst, *Every Secret Thing*, p. 187 (breaking down guns).

67. *Trial Transcript*, pp. 84 (Matthews testimony), 139 (Thomas Padden testimony).

68. Alexander, *Anyone's Daughter*, p. 311.

69. "Fromme Meets Press," *Sacramento Bee*, 19 September 1975, p. A3 ("earth polluters"); Patricia O'Brien, "Women with a Gun," *Chicago Sun-Times*, 25 September 1975, pp. 81, 136.

70. "Ford Escapes Uninjured as Woman Pulls Trigger," *Sacramento Bee*, 23 September 1975, p. 1; "Who Is the Woman Who Shot at the President?" *Boston Globe*, 23 September 1975, p. 3; Helen Thomas (for United Press International), "President Escapes Assassin's Bullet," *Boston Globe*, 23 September 1975, p. 1; Wendell Davis and Mary Walton, "Background: Sara Moore's Many Names Dot an Elusive Trail," *Boston Globe*, 24 September 1975, p. 9; Ellen Hume (for the *Los Angeles Times*), "I'm Glad He Didn't Die," *Boston Globe*, 23 September 1975, p. 14 ("forge . . . unity"); Lester, *Girl in a Box*, pp. 69, 79–80.

71. O'Brien, "Women with a Gun," p. 81; Martin F. Nolan, "A Mobile Shooting Gallery," *Boston Globe*, 25 September 1975, p. 30 ("deranged"); editorial, *Indianapolis News*, 25 September 1975, *Editorials on File*, 6:1139; editorial, *Pittsburgh Post-Gazette*, 20 September 1975, *Editorials on* File, 6:1143 ("least liberated"); *Sacramento Bee*, 23 September 1975, p. 1 (juxtaposed psychiatric stories); *Montgom-*

ery Advertiser, 24 September 1975, p. 1 (all on one page). The growth of the women's movement took place at the same time as a rise in the female crime rate. See Schuetz, *Logic of Women on Trial*, p. 163.

72. Laura Browder, *Her Best Shot: Women and Guns in America* (Chapel Hill: University of North Carolina Press, 2006), pp. 136 (Stern), 156 (Shakur), 137 ("public forum"), 180–81 (feminism), 182 ("sexual awakening"), 185 ("cultural nightmare"). Natasha Zaretsky perceptively argues that one of the most widespread cultural critiques of the 1970s, the association of the decade with narcissism, was implicitly a critique of feminist ambivalence about motherhood. Although I have found no evidence explicitly linking the SLA or Patty Hearst to the narcissism debate, their apparent lack of interest in reproduction made them vulnerable to the accusation. See Zaretsky, *No Direction Home: The American Family and the Fear of National Decline, 1968–1980* (Chapel Hill: University of North Carolina Press, 2007), pp. 197–99.

73. Editorial, *Chicago Daily Defender*, 23 September 1975, *Editorials on File*, 6:1144; editorial, *Newsday*, 20 September 1975, *Editorials on File*, 6:1145; editorial, *Chicago Sun-Times*, 20 September 1975, *Editorials on File*, 6:1145; Bill Granger, "At SLA Death Site, They Doubt Patty to Do Time," *Chicago Sun-Times*, 21 September 1975, p. 8.

74. Jenkins, *Decade of Nightmares*, p. 96.

75. Editorial, *The State* (Columbia, SC), 25 September 1975, *Editorials on* File, 6:1141; editorial, *Charleston Gazette*, 20 September 1975, *Editorials on File*, 6:1140; editorial, *Springfield* (MA) *Union*, 20 September 1975, *Editorials on File*, 6:1144.

76. "Judge's Action in Hearst Case Affirms Pattern," *Montgomery Advertiser*, 13 April 1976, p. 5; Dave Smith, "The Many Trials of Patty Hearst," *Los Angeles Times*, 27 February 1976, sect. 4, p. 1; "Judge Revokes Patty's Bail; Recites Risks," *Montgomery Advertiser*, 20 September 1975, p. 1. Judge Carter had known Randolph Hearst since 1960, when he was a dinner guest at the family's Hillsborough home. "I've known Randy Hearst for years," he told the *New York Times* as he was preparing for Patty's trial. " I saw all those kids when they were youngsters. Heavens, you can't be around California and not know Randy. You can't be in public life and not know Randy." Lacey Fosburgh, "Judge in Hearst Case," *New York Times*, 25 September 1975.

77. Alexander, *Anyone's Daughter*, p. 39.

78. Alexander, *Anyone's Daughter*, pp. 50, 27, 145, 29 ("barracuda"). Bancroft earned a BA from Swarthmore in 1960. Bailey's background is drawn from several Internet sites, including http://www.law.umkc.edu/faculty/projects/ftrials/mylai/myl_bbailey.htm ("extreme egocentricity") (accessed 12 February 2008). On David P. Davis Jr., see http://www.orrick.com/lawyers/Bio.asp?ID=161276 (accessed 21 February 2008).

79. *Trial Transcript*, pp. 1–6 ("taints" is on p. 6), 98.

80. Ibid., pp. 6–8.

81. Alexander, *Anyone's Daughter*, p. 145 (clothes); *Trial Transcript*, pp. 151–58 (Hearst testimony); "Mail to Miss Hearst Becoming Sympathetic, Attorneys Report," *Los Angeles Times*, 14 February 1976, sect. 1, p. 25.

82. *Trial Transcript* (Hearst testimony), pp. 176 (FBI), 177 ("would be killed"), 178 ("death"), 186 ("urban guerrilla").

83. Ibid., p. 189.

84. Ibid., p. 190.

85. Ibid., p. 201.

86. Ibid., p. 201 ("Tania Interview" excerpt); Colin Greer, *The Great School Legend* (New York: Viking Press, 1972); Joel H. Spring, *Education and the Rise of the Corporate State* (Boston: Beacon Press, 1972); Herbert I. Schiller, *The Mind Managers* (Boston: Beacon Press, 1973); Ivan Illich, *Deschooling Society* (New York: Harper & Row, 1971).

87. Christopher Castiglia, *Bound and Determined: Captivity, Culture-Crossing, and White Womanhood from Mary Rowlandson to Patty Hearst* (Chicago: University of Chicago Press, 1996), pp. 87–105.

88. *Trial Transcript* (Hearst testimony), p. 214.

89. Ibid., p. 211.

90. Ibid., pp. 228–29.

91. *Trial Transcript* (Hall testimony), pp. 233–34; Alexander, *Anyone's Daughter*, p. 237 (Catherine Hearst).

92. *Trial Transcript*, pp. 510 (Bailey, Browning), 599 (Carter on duress); Lyle Denniston, "The Hearst Defense," *Boston Evening Globe*, 22 September 1975, p. 2.

93. Donald T. Lunde and Thomas E. Wilson, "Brainwashing as a Defense to Criminal Liability: Patty Hearst Revisited," *Criminal Law Bulletin* 13 (September/October 1977): 342.

94. *Trial Transcript* (West testimony), pp. 248–49, 250–51 (DDD, "heroic"), 252 ("terrible fear"), 256–57 ("numb with terror," "be killed"). On the American reaction to the twenty-one POWs who refused repatriation—because, it was said, they had been "brainwashed"—see Adam J. Zweiback, "The 21 'Turncoat GIs': Nonrepatriations and the Political Culture of the Korean War," *Historian* 2 (Winter 1998): 345–62, and Catherine Lutz, "Epistemology of the Bunker: The Brainwashed and Other New Subjects of Permanent War," in *Inventing the Psychological: Toward a Cultural History of Emotional Life in America*, ed. Joel Pfister and Nancy Schnog (New Haven: Yale University Press, 1997), pp. 245–67.

95. *Trial Transcript* (West testimony), pp. 259–60 ("enemy hands," "dissociative features"), 253 ("survivor syndrome"), 261 ("staying alive").

96. Jozsef Cardinal Mindszenty, *Memoirs* (New York: Macmillan, 1974), pp. 92 ("outfit"), 95, 98, 103, 114 (*Yellow Book*), 126, 135; *Trial Transcript* (West testimony), pp. 251 ("Mindszenty look"—misspelled as "Myzenti" in transcript), 253.

97. *Trial Transcript* (West testimony), pp. 263–64, 269 ("urban guerrilla"), 288, 264 (West's bias), 267 (Korean War pilots), 268 ("woke me").

98. Ibid., p. 273.

99. Ibid., pp. 263, 281 ("schoolgirl"), 278 ("nun," "sarcasm"), 281 (LSD).

100. Ibid., pp. 282–83.

101. *Trial Transcript* (Orne testimony), pp. 298–99 ("traumatic neurosis"), 293 ("tests are given"), 292, 298 (extreme reaction). Orne took the stand on February 25. In a *Time* article, "The Psychology of Homecoming," a psychoanalyst described the emotional syndrome produced by captivity as "a zombie reaction." Andreas Killen, *1973 Nervous Breakdown: Watergate, Warhol, and the Birth of Post-Sixties America* (New York: Bloomsbury, 2006), p. 82.

102. *Trial Transcript*, p. 309 (Orne testimony).

103. Ibid., p. 310.

104. *Trial Transcript* (Lifton testimony), pp. 314, 317–20 (process); 322 (numbing of emotions).

105. Ibid., pp. 320–21.

106. Ibid., pp. 329 ("own kind"), 334 (Occam's Razor).

107. "Hearst Trial Fireworks Expected Again," *Montgomery Advertiser*, 8 March 1976, p. 3 (description of Fort); *Trial Transcript* (Fort testimony), pp. 399, 424, 466, 427, 419, 420 ("sick position"), 435 (concentration camps).

108. *Trial Transcript* (Fort testimony), pp. 441 ("fulfilled life"), 431, 436 ("voluntary member"); Alexander, *Anyone's Daughter*, p. 370 (green suit).

109. *Trial Transcript* (Fort testimony), pp. 426–27 ("attitude change"), 439–40 ("actions"), 440, 437 ("die for"), 432–33 ("independent," "relief of boredom"); *Trial Transcript* (Randolph and Catherine Hearst testimony), pp. 560, 572.

110. *Trial Transcript* (Fort testimony), pp. 432, 424 ("Jesus Freaks"), 434 ("self-esteem"), 433 (middle-class women), 437 ("broad social movement"), 435 ("commitment"), 436 ("voluntary member"), 439 ("status"); Associated Press, "Witness Calls Patty 'Queen' of SLA," *Montgomery Advertiser*, 9 March 1976, p. 5.

111. Alexander, *Anyone's Daughter*, pp. 399–400 (Kozol description); *Trial Transcript* (Kozol testimony), pp. 486, 488 ("Montreal"), 489 ("intimate"). The transcript reads "mashing in the streets." Kozol took the stand on March 10.

112. *Trial Transcript* (Kozol testimony), pp. 516.

113. Ibid., p. 517.

114. Ibid., pp. 518 ("depressed and unhappy"), 520 ("dishes"), 519 ("liberation of women").

115. Ibid., pp. 523 ("freedom"), 520 ("working people," "subtle hostility"), 520–21 ("no place to go").

116. Ibid., p. 521; emphasis added.

117. Peter N. Carroll, *It Seemed Like Nothing Happened: The Tragedy and Promise of America in the 1970s* (New York: Holt, Rinehart and Winston, 1982), pp. 278–80; Killen, *1973 Nervous Breakdown*, pp. 55–76 (Loud family).

118. *Trial Transcript* (Fort testimony), p. 437.

119. *Trial Transcript* (Kozol testimony), pp. 533, 534 ("exam," "rebelliousness"), 532–33 ("free to go"), 535 (Mindszenty).

120. Ibid., pp. 523 ("accelerated"), 524, 531 ("own heart"), 530 ("impressions," speech patterns).

121. Ibid., p. 533.

122. *Trial Transcript* (Fort testimony), pp. 446 (press release), 451 (book), 449 ("Bald").

123. Ibid., pp. 467, 462, 465, 402 ("eyebrows"), 446 ("media").

124. Ibid., pp. 472 (Fort's ignorance), 459 ("fell over one"), 473 ("Mr. Manson," quoted from the Manson trial transcript).

125. *Trial Transcript* (Padden, Meighan, and Callahan testimony), pp. 536–37.

126. Alexander, *Anyone's Daughter*, p. 449.

127. *Trial Transcript* (Browning closing), pp. 580 ("voluntary"), 581 ("swinging the weapon"), 582 (in the bank, "film," "no hesitation," "nobody").

128. Ibid., p. 587 ("common sense"). For a similar view on the "facts" issue, see Nancy Isenberg, "Not 'Anyone's Daughter': Patty Hearst and the Postmodern Legal Subject," *American Quarterly* 52 (December 2000): 641.

129. *Trial Transcript* (Browning closing), pp. 582 ("circumstantial"), 584 ("we called her"), 583 (all other material).

130. Ibid., pp. 586–87.

131. Ibid., p. 585.

132. Ibid., pp. 584 ("unscrew top"), 585 (other quotations).

133. Ibid., pp. 587 (litany of false statements), 588 ("incredible"), 589 ("little stone face").

134. Ibid., p. 589.

135. Ibid.

136. *Trial Transcript* (Bailey closing), pp. 592 ("perplexed"), 591, 593 (Mason).

137. Ibid., pp. 590 ("rich girl," survival versus freedom, "psychopaths"), 592 (please those outside, "not flaming liberal," Chicago Eight).

138. Ibid., p. 590.

139. Ibid., pp. 589 ("peripheral matters"), 590 (affidavit, Mel's), 592.

140. Ibid., pp. 589, 591 ("bells on," "habitual liar," "cut his legs off"), 590 (Mindszenty, POWs).

141. Ibid., p. 589; Piers Paul Read, *Alive: The Story of the Andes Survivors* (New York: Lippincott, Williams & Wilkins, 1974); Stephen D. Becker, *A Covenant with Death* (New York: Atheneum, 1965).

142. *Trial Transcript* (Bailey closing), pp. 591, 592.

143. Ibid., pp. 591 ("bullet"), 593 ("wanted to survive"); Hearst, *Every Secret Thing*, p. 430; McLellan and Avery, *Voices of Guns*, p. 28 (Hallinan). On Bailey's handling of the defense, see editorial, "A Single Standard," *Detroit News*, 23 March 1976, p. 6-B; John Cogley, "Hearst Case Leaves a Free-Will Puzzle," *Los Angeles Times*, 28 March 1976, sect. 8, p. 1; editorial, *Charleston Gazette*, 23 March 1976, *Editorials on File*, 7:469; Alexander, *Anyone's Daughter*, pp. 518–19.

144. "The Jury," (Portland) *Maine Sunday Telegram*, 21 March 1976, pp. 1A, 8A; Alexander, *Anyone's Daughter*, p. 524; *Los Angeles Times*, 25 March 1976, sect. 2, p. 6.

145. *Trial Transcript*, p. 599; Ronald Koziol, "Patty More Valuable as Witness Than Prisoner, Mother Says," *Salt Lake Tribune*, 26 March 1976, p. 14A (Catherine Hearst). A letter to the *Los Angeles Times* made the same point, while misunderstanding Carter's instructions. See Bernadette Amaker, *Los Angeles Times*, 25 March 1976, sect. 2, p. 6. Carter's perspective on the duress defense had become apparent soon after Patty's arrest, when he told attorney Terence Hallinan that the effort to link the kidnapping with the bank robbery was "a kind of mental diversion." Denniston, "The Hearst Defense," p. 2. According to Lunde and Wilson, the legal standard for a judgment of duress was "a standard of personal courage," under which "the accused must demonstrate that the coercive force was resisted at least to the point where a person of ordinary firmness, fortitude, and courage would have capitulated." They describe the "fatal flaw" in the Hearst case as her "failure to take advantage of opportunities to escape the coercion of her captors" after the Hibernia robbery. Lunde and Wilson, "Brainwashing as a Defense," pp. 355, 357.

146. "The Jury," *Maine Sunday Telegram*, 21 March 1976, p. 1A (crocheting); "Patty Hearst Guilty of Bank Robbery," *Denver Post*, 21 March 1976, pp. 1, 5; "Patricia Hearst Found Guilty," *Montgomery Advertiser*, 21 March 1976, p. 1A; "Patri-

cia Hearst Guilty," *Maine Sunday Telegram*, 21 March 1976, p. 1 (pat on back); *Trial Transcript*, p. 602 (verdict).

147. "Patty Found Guilty," *Indianapolis Star*, 21 March 1976, p. 1 ("Oh, my God," "white with shock"); Wallace Turner, "Miss Hearst Is Convicted on Bank Robbery Charges," *New York Times*, 21 March 1976, p. 1 (forehead); "Patricia Hearst Guilty," *Maine Sunday Telegram*, 21 March 1976, p. 1 ("Oh Christ"); Hearst, *Every Secret Thing*, p. 431 ("never had a chance").

148. *Public Papers of the Presidents of the United States: Jimmy Carter*, (Washington, DC: Government Printing Office, 1980), 1:217; "Opposition to Freeing of Miss Hearst Voiced," *New York Times*, 2 February 1979, p. 12; photo and caption, "Patty Home," *Indianapolis Star*, 2 February 1979, p. 1; "Patty Grins, Jokes, Goes Home to Mother," *Indianapolis Star*, 2 February 1979, p. 3 (medallion); "Father's Newspaper Sees 'Injustice' in Hearst Case," *New York Times*, 5 February 1979, p. 12; editorial, "Freeing the Victim," *Portland* (Maine) *Press Herald*, 1 February 1979, p. 12. See also "Five-Year Nightmare Over for Patty Hearst," *Buffalo News*, 1 February 1979, p. 1, and letters to editor, *Los Angeles Times*, 17 May 1977, sect. 2, p. 6.

149. Lacey Fosburgh, "Hearst Jurors Hoped to Believe," *New York Times*, 22 March 1974, pp. 1, 42 ("didn't believe her," "outweighed by the evidence"); "Bailey Says Miss Hearst May Get Modest Sentence," *Minneapolis Tribune Star*, 23 March 1976, p. 10A (Grim, Crabbe).

150. Fosburgh, "Hearst Jurors," p. 42.

151. Diane Johnson, *Terrorists and Novelists* (New York: Alfred A. Knopf, 1982), pp. 232–33. The book contains a chapter on the Hearst trial.

152. Editorial, *Richmond News Leader*, 22 March 1976, *Editorials on File*, 7: 466; Robert F. Tomasson, "Public's Feelings Strong for and against Verdict," *New York Times*, 21 March 1976, p. 46 ("the right verdict"); editorial, *Detroit Free Press*, 24 March 1976, p. 6-A; *Charleston* (West Virginia) *Gazette*, 25 March 1976, *Editorials on File*, 7:469. See also "Justice Served in Hearst Case," editorial, *Denver Post*, 24 March 1976, p. 16; "Guilty: So Be It," editorial, *Chattanooga Times*, 24 March 1976, p. 8; editorial, *Salt Lake Tribune*, 23 March 1976, *Editorials on File*, 7:468; editorial, *Cincinnati Post*, 23 March 1976, *Editorials on File*, 7:469; "Case Decided on the Evidence," editorial, *Topeka Daily Capital*, 25 March 1976, p. 4; Malcolm B. Johnson, "Patty's Conviction Fit Nation," *Miami Herald*, 25 March 1976, p. 7A.

153. Typescript of Reagan tape 78-08-A3, 5 June 1978, transcribed in *Reagan's Path to Victory*, ed. Kiron K. Skinner, Annelise Anderson, and Martin Anderson (New York: Simon & Schuster, 2004), pp. 305–7. The handwritten version is at the Ronald Reagan Presidential Library, Simi Valley, California.

154. Royko, "'If Patty Isn't Guilty, Why'd She Do It'" ("kidnaped" is spelled with one *p* in the original). See also letters to editor, *Los Angeles Times*, 25 March 1976, sect. 2, p. 6, and 14 October 1976, sect. 2, p. 6, and "Students on Hearst Trial," *Denver Post*, 23 March 1976, p. 19.

155. Editorial, *Cincinnati Post*, 23 March 1976, *Editorials on File*, 7:469; editorial, *Kansas City Star*, 24 March 1976, *Editorials on File*, 7:469.

156. Editorial, *Des Moines Register*, 23 March 1976, p. 6A; Robert Jay Lifton, "On the Hearst Trial," *New York Times*, 16 April 1976, p. 27.

157. Phil Kerby, "Above All, Patty Was a Victim," *Los Angeles Times*, 30 September 1976, sect. 2, p. 1; letters to editor, *Los Angeles Times*, 14 October 1976,

sect. 2, p. 6. See also editorial, *Rochester* (NY) *Democrat Chronicle*, 23 March 1976, *Editorials on File*, 7:467.

158. John Teets, "PhotOpinion," *Chicago Sun-Times*, 24 March 1976, p. 60 (charm, escape); editorial, *Rochester Democrat Chronicle*, 23 March 1976, *Editorials on File*, 7:467; editorial, *Saginaw News*, 23 March 1976, *Editorials on File*, 7:465 (escape, Fifth); "Patty's Clear Guilt," editorial, *Arizona Republic*, 23 March 1976, p. A-6 (charm, escape, Fifth); editorial, *Tulsa World*, 23 March 1976, *Editorials on File*, 7:466 (Fifth, escape, charm, Tobin tape); editorial, *Richmond News Leader*, 22 March 1976, *Editorials on File*, 7:466 (escape, Fifth, charm).

159. "Case Decided on the Evidence," editorial, *Topeka Daily Capital*, 25 March 1976, p. 4; letter, Bruce Wilson to *Salt Lake Tribune*, 22 March 1976, p. 14; editorial, *Montreal Star*, 23 March 1976, *Editorials on File*, 7:467; "More Confusion Than Fact," editorial, *Salt Lake Tribune*, 13 March 1976, p. 10 ("inexact art"); editorial, *Richmond News Leader*, 22 March 1976, *Editorials on* File, 7:466 ("rationalizing"); Malcolm B. Johnson (editor, *Tallahassee Democrat*), "Patty's Conviction Fit Nation," *Miami Herald*, 25 March 1976, p. 7A ("rest of us").

160. "Patty's Clear Guilt," editorial, *Arizona Republic*, 23 March 1976, p. A6; "The Patty Hearst Verdict," editorial, *Detroit Free Press*, 24 March 1976, p. 6A; editorial, *Baltimore Sun*, 23 March 1976, *Editorials on File*, 7:466; editorial, *Chicago Tribune*, 23 March 1976, *Editorials on File*, 7:467; "Students on Hearst Trial," *Denver Post*, 23 March 1976, p. 19. See also Walter Reich, "Brainwashing, Psychiatry and the Law," *New York Times*, 29 May 1976, p. 23. The decision in *Miranda v. Arizona*, 384 U.S. 436 (1966), held that before questioning a suspect about the possible commission of a crime, law enforcement officials must inform the suspect of what came to be known as "Miranda rights," which consist of the rights to remain silent and to have an attorney present.

161. This paragraph is adapted from Jenkins, *Decade of Nightmares*, pp. 134–43.

162. Editorial, *Washington Star*, 23 March 1976, *Editorials on File*, 7:468 ("shallow determinism," "God-given free will"); editorial, *Cincinnati Post*, 3 March 1976, *Editorials on File*, 7:469 ("victim"); editorial, *Rochester Democrat Chronicle*, 23 March 1976, *Editorials on File*, 7:467; Reich, "Brainwashing."

163. John Cogley, "Hearst Case Leaves a Free-Will Puzzle," *Los Angeles Times*, 28 March 1976, sect. 8, p. 1.

164. "Justice Served in Hearst Case," editorial, *Denver Post*, 24 March 1976, p. 16; "Fair Verdict on Patty," editorial, *Buffalo News*, 22 March 1976, p. 14; "Miss Hearst Is Convicted on Bank Robbery Charges," *New York Times*, 21 March 1976, p. 46.

165. Editorial, *Arkansas Democrat*, 10 April 1976, *Editorials on File*, 7:466 (need to "protest"); editorial, *Seattle Times*, 23 March 1976, *Editorials on File*, 7:467 ("revolutionary rhetoric," "establishment"); editorial, *Richmond News Leader*, 22 March 1976, *Editorials on File*, 7:466 ("urban guerrilla").

166. Editorial, *Richmond News Leader*, 22 March 1976, *Editorials on File*, 7:466; editorial, *Winston-Salem Journal*, 23 March 1976, *Editorials on File*, 7:464.

Reading Patty Hearst

1. Mark Crispin Miller, "*Barry Lyndon* Reconsidered," *Georgia Review* 30 (winter 1976): 827–54. On *Badlands*, see Andreas Killen, *1973 Nervous Breakdown:*

Watergate, Warhol, and the Birth of Post-Sixties America (New York: Bloomsbury, 2006), pp. 190–92. The quotations are from the film. The art world went through something similar, abandoning the optimism and objectivity of modernism for a variety of more personal and intimate forms and methods. See Kim Levin, "Farewell to Modernism," in *Beyond Modernism: Essays on Art from the '70s and '80s* (New York: Harper & Row, 1988), pp. 3–12.

2. John F. Kasson, *Rudeness & Civility: Manners in Nineteenth-Century Urban America* (New York: Hill and Wang, 1990), pp. 28–33, 82–86.

3. Warren I. Susman, "'Personality' and the Making of Twentieth-Century Culture," in *New Directions in American Intellectual History*, ed. John Higham and Paul K. Conkin (Baltimore: Johns Hopkins University Press, 1979), pp. 212–26 (quotation on p. 220); Karen Halttunen, *Confidence Men and Painted Women: A Study of Middle-Class Culture in America, 1830–1870* (New Haven: Yale University Press, 1982), p. 237n28; Joel Pfister, "Glamorizing the Psychological: The Politics of the Performances of Modern Psychological Identities," in *Inventing the Psychological: Toward a Cultural History of Emotional Life in America*, ed. Joel Pfister and Nancy Schnog (New Haven, CT: Yale University Press, 1997), pp. 174, 176.

4. Tom Carson, "David Bowie," in *The Rolling Stone Illustrated History of Rock & Roll*, ed. Jim Miller, rev. ed. (New York: Random House, 1980), pp. 386–87.

5. Editorial, *Arizona Republic*, 23 March 1976, reprinted in *Editorials on File*, vol. 7 (New York: Facts on File, 1976), p. 465.

6. Nancy Kay Turner, "Cindy Sherman," at http://artscenecal.com/ArticlesFile/Archive/Articles1997/Articles1197/CShermanA.html; "The Complete *Untitled Film Stills*," http://moma.org/exhibitions/1997/sherman/index.html; Amada Cruz, "Movies, Monstrosities, and Masks: Twenty Years of Cindy Sherman," in "Cindy Sherman: Retrospective," http://www.masters-of-photography.com/S/sherman/sherman_articles3.html; *Consider the Alternatives: 20 Years of Contemporary Art at Hallwalls*, ed. Ronald Ehmke with Elizabeth Licata (Buffalo, New York: Hallwalls Contemporary Arts Center, 1996), pp. 18, 24, 41. Sherman and Hearst played small roles in John Waters's film *Pecker* (1998). See Gerald Peary, "Cindy, Patty, and John: A Day on the Set of *Pecker*," *Boston Phoenix*, August 6–13 1998, http://bostonphoenix.com/archive/movies/98/08/06/PECKER.html (all URLs accessed 12 February 2008).

7. Roy F. Baumeister, *Identity: Culture Change and the Struggle for the Self* (New York: Oxford University Press, 1986), pp. 42 ("authentic individuality"), 92 (celebrity), 121. The book contains a chapter on brainwashing, seen as a way to undermine or change identity. See also Robert G. Dunn, *Identity Crises: A Social Critique of Modernity* (Minneapolis: University of Minnesota Press, 1998), pp. 22–23. Andreas Killen notes the relationship between name changes (which characterized SLA members) and the culture of the celebrity in the Terrence Malick film *Badlands*, released in October 1973. Killen, *1973 Nervous Breakdown*, pp. 187–94.

8. "Situation vs. Personality Debate," http://www.wilderdom.com/personality/L6-3SituationVsPersonality.html (accessed 12 February 2008); Walter Mischel, *Personality and Assessment* (New York: Wiley, 1968).

9. Philip G. Zimbardo, "A Situationist Perspective on the Psychology of Evil: Understanding How Good People Are Transformed into Perpetrators," in *The Social Psychology of Good and Evil*, ed. Arthur G. Miller (New York: Guilford Press, 2004), p. 40; *The Trial of Patty Hearst* (San Francisco: Great Fidelity Press, 1976), pp. 252, 570, hereafter referred to as *Trial Transcript*.

10. Lasch, *The Minimal Self: Psychic Survival in Troubled Times* (New York: W. W. Norton, 1984), p. 15; Peter N. Carroll, *It Seemed Like Nothing Happened: The Tragedy and Promise of America in the 1970s* (New York: Holt, Rinehart and Winston), pp. 297–300; Robert Phillip Kolker, *A Cinema of Loneliness: Penn, Kubrick, Scorsese, Spielberg, Altman*, 2nd ed. (1980; New York: Oxford University Press, 1988), p. 181.

11. Killen, *1973 Nervous Breakdown*, pp. 127–29 (*Sybil*). On late-twentieth-century filmic images of the psychiatrist, see Dennis Palumbo, "Shrinkage," *Written By: The Magazine of the Writers Guild of America, West* 10 (November 2006): 50–52. On post-Vietnam films, see William Palmer, *The Films of the Eighties: A Social History* (Carbondale: Southern Illinois University Press, 1993), esp. pp. 87–90.

12. Jesse F. Ballenger, *Self, Senility, and Alzheimer's Disease in Modern America* (Baltimore: Johns Hopkins University Press, 2006), pp. 135 ("worst"), 109 ("century"), 136, 153 ("modern America").

13. Joan Jacobs Brumberg, *Fasting Girls: The Emergence of Anorexia Nervosa as a Modern Disease* (Cambridge, MA: Harvard University Press, 1988), pp. 3, 8, 10 ("disease of the 1970s"), 2 ("symbolic language"), 271 ("personal dreams," "dutiful daughters"); Jacinta O. A. Tan, Tony Hope, and Anne Stewart, "Anorexia Nervosa and Personal Identity: The Accounts of Patients and Their Parents," *International Journal of Law and Psychiatry* 26 (2003): 533–48 (available online in the Science direct database; the quotation is in section 7.1).

14. This portrait is a composite, culled from Natasha Zaretsky, *No Direction Home: The American Family and the Fear of National Decline, 1968–1980* (Chapel Hill: University of North Carolina Press, 2007), pp. 184–85, 188–91, 206; *The Search for the Self: Selected Writings of Heinz Kohut, 1950–1978*, ed. Paul H. Ornstein, 2 vols. (New York: International Universities Press, 1978), 2: 620, 627, 636–38 ("narcissistic rage"), 846, 886; and Christopher Lasch, *The Culture of Narcissism: American Life in an Age of Diminishing Expectations* (New York: W. W. Norton, 1978), pp. xvi, 10–11, 21, 25, 42.

15. Lasch, *Culture of Narcissism*, pp. 94, xiii ("crisis," "despair"), xiv, 5, 21, 49, 51 ("without faith").

16. Lasch, *Culture of Narcissism*, pp. 175, 164, 167, 170, 175; Kohut, *Search for the Self*, pp. 649,779 ("bridge cards").

17. Vin McLellan and Paul Avery, *The Voices of Guns* (New York: G. P. Putnam's Sons, 1977), p. 41 (Yoshimura letter).

18. Patricia Campbell Hearst, with Alvin Moscow, *Every Secret Thing* (Garden City, NY: Doubleday, 1982), pp. 325 (quotations), 343 (on guns), 187 (weapons drills), 292 (dislike of exercise).

19. Shana Alexander, *Anyone's Daughter* (New York: Viking Press, 1979), pp. 421 (Regents), 78–80 (Singer report).

20. Janice Schuetz, *The Logic of Women on Trial: Case Studies of Popular American Trials* (Carbondale: Southern Illinois University Press, 1994), pp. 164–67, 170 (on disguise as identity change).

21. Christopher Castiglia, *Bound and Determined: Captivity, Culture-Crossing, and White Womanhood from Mary Rowlandson to Patty Hearst* (Chicago: University of Chicago Press, 1996), p. 98.

22. Killen, *1973 Nervous Breakdown*, p. 9.

23. See Stacy Thompson, *Punk Productions: Unfinished Business* (Albany: SUNY Press, 2004), pp. 1–32. Hell is quoted in Killen, *1973 Nervous Breakdown*, p. 155.

24. Nancy Isenberg, "Not 'Anyone's Daughter': Patty Hearst and the Postmodern Legal Subject," *American Quarterly* 52 (December 2000): 642 ("simulated"), 663, 656, 655 ("gender script"), 662 ("imagine a whole"), 667.

25. Ballenger, *Self, Senility, and Alzheimer's Disease*, p. 152.

26. On the Peoples Temple, see David Chidester, *Salvation and Suicide: An Interpretation of Jim Jones, the Peoples Temple, and Jonestown* (Bloomington: Indiana University Press, 1988). Robert W. Dellinger, *Cults and Kids: A Study of Coercion* (Boys Town, NE: Boys Town Center, n.d.), p. 1 (Singer); Margaret Thaler Singer, "Coming Out of the Cults," *Psychology Today* 12 (January 1979): 72–82. In their essay on brainwashing, Lunde and Wilson cite the conversion methods employed by the Moonies and those used to extract propaganda statements from captured American sailors of the U.S.S. *Pueblo* as examples of coercive persuasion. Donald T. Lunde and Thomas E. Wilson, "Brainwashing as a Defense to Criminal Liability: Patty Hearst Revisited," *Criminal Law Bulletin* 13 (September/October 1977): 351.

27. Killen, *1973 Nervous Breakdown*, p. 129.

28. Daniel Boorstin, *The Image: or What Happened to the American Dream* (New York: Atheneum, 1962), p. 57 (emphasis in original); Lasch, *Culture of Narcissism*, pp. 78–79 ("politics and spectacle"), 75–76, 82–84; Todd Gitlin, *The Whole World Is Watching: Mass Media in the Making & Unmaking of the New Left* (Berkeley: University of California Press, 1980), pp. 176, 146–47; Zaretsky, *No Direction Home*, p. 206.

29. Joshua Gamson, *Claims to Fame: Celebrity in Contemporary America* (Berkeley: University of California Press, 1994), p. 43 (*People*, *Newsweek*); Ellis Cashmore, *Celebrity/Culture* (New York: Routledge, 2006), pp. 190–91 ("plasticity of people," Louds). The Warhol quotation is among several at Wikipedia (search under "15 Minutes of Fame").

30. Samantha Barbas, *Movie Crazy: Fans, Stars, and the Cult of Celebrity* (New York: Palgrave, 2001), pp. 4–6, 82, 101, 108, 123, 140.

31. Stuart Ewen, *All Consuming Images: The Politics of Style in Contemporary Culture* (New York: Basic Books, 1988), p. 94 ("dream of identity"); Boorstin, *Image*, pp. 60–61. See also Richard Schickel, *Intimate Strangers: The Culture of Celebrity* (Garden City, NY: Doubleday, 1985), pp. 93, 103.

32. *The Stepford Wives* (1975), screenplay by William Goldman; Ira Levin, *The Stepford Wives* (New York: Random House, 1972), pp. 113–17; "Genetic Engineering," *Newsweek*, 79 (May 15, 1972), p. 72. Margaret Atwood's novel *The Handmaid's Tale* (1986) takes up a similar theme.

33. David Herzberg, "'The Pill You Love Can Turn on You': Feminism, Tranquilizers, and the Valium Panic of the 1970s," *American Quarterly* 58 (March 2006): 79–103, esp. 87 ("she could even be you"), 89–91 (Kennedy, Ford, other examples).

34. Herzberg, "The Pill," pp. 84 ("disease"), 99 (Reagan).

35. Nick Cull, "*The Exorcist*," *History Today* 50 (May 2000): 46–51, esp. 48; Timothy Paxton with David Todarello, "The Exorcist Made Me Do It! Possession Films of the 1970s," http://users.aol.com/monsterint/1996/possession.html

(accessed 23 February 2008), originally published in *Monster! International* (#3); Alexander, *Anyone's Daughter*, pp. 363 ("exorcism"), 485 ("devil"), 274. Christopher Castiglia takes up *The Exorcist* and the Hearst kidnapping and suggests the "metaphoric parallel between captivity and satanic possession" in *Bound and Determined*, pp. 87–89 (quotation p. 88). Flip Wilson's character Geraldine made the line "The Devil made me do it" into a national catchphrase on the *Flip Wilson Show*, which aired from 1970 through 1974.

36. Alexander, *Anyone's Daughter*, p. 539 ("could not help her"); Susan Sontag, "The Imagination of Disaster," in *Film Theory and Criticism: Introductory Readings*, ed. Gerald Mast and Marshall Cohen, 2nd ed. (New York: Oxford University Press, 1979), p. 499, an essay first published in *Against Interpretation* (1965). The archetypal artistic figure of the decade after 1965 was Andy Warhol, whose persona was regularly described as zombie like: pale, bored, and affectless, a living cadaver. Killen, *1973 Nervous Breakdown*, p. 146.

37. William Graebner, "America's *Poseidon Adventure*: A Nation in Existential Despair," in *America in the Seventies*, ed. Beth Bailey and David Farber (Lawrence: University Press of Kansas, 2004), pp. 165–68. Peter Dendle, in *The Zombie Movie Encyclopedia* (London: McFarland & Company, 2001), labels the period 1968–1983 the "golden age" of the zombie film. Between 1969 and 1977, more than thirty zombie films appeared in the United States and other countries (pp. 7–8, 12 ["zombie just is"]).

38. Harlow M. Huckabee, *Lawyers, Psychiatrists and Criminal Law: Cooperation or Chaos?* (Springfield, IL: Charles C. Thomas, 1980), pp. 8 (Pollack), 9 (Pound), 103 (Menninger).

39. Huckabee, *Lawyers, Psychiatrists*, pp. 15, 31 ("compulsion"); William Ryan, *Blaming the Victim*, rev. ed. (1971; New York: Vintage Books, 1976), pp. 7, 15, 28–29.

40. Kirsten Fermaglich, *American Dreams and Nazi Nightmares: Early Holocaust Consciousness and Liberal America, 1957–1965* (Waltham, MA: Brandeis University Press, 2006), pp. 22, 26–29. See also Daryl Michael Scott, *Contempt and Pity: Social Policy and the Image of the Damaged Black Psyche, 1880–1996* (Chapel Hill: University of North Carolina Press,1997).

41. Betty Friedan, *The Feminine Mystique* (1963; New York: Dell, 1973), pp. 296 ("childlike," "comfortable"), 294 ("walked to their own death"); Fermaglich, *American Dreams*, pp. 58, 60, 75.

42. Friedan, *Feminine Mystique*, pp. 293 ("sense of human identity"), 322 ("crisis," work), 324 ("death of self," "living death").

43. Fermaglich, *American Dreams*, pp. 88–89 (Eichmann), 133 ("extreme situations"), 85–86, 91 (Milgram experiments), 124–26, 132–33, 141–44 (Lifton).

44. John W. Blassingame, *The Slave Community: Plantation Life in the Antebellum South* (New York: Oxford University Press, 1972), pp. 225–26, 71, 209, 99, 107, 215–16. The ASALH papers, and other writings on *The Slave Community*, are gathered in *Revisiting Blassingame's "The Slave Community": The Scholars Respond*, ed. Al-Tony Gilmore (Westport, CT: Greenwood Press, 1978); see esp. p. xiii.

45. Fermaglich, *American Dreams*, pp. 67–69, 52–53, 80–81, 113 (Bell), 158, 156 ("not a victim"); Alyson M. Cole, *The Cult of True Victimhood: From the War on Welfare to the War on Terror* (Stanford, CA: Stanford University Press, 2007), p. 71 (feminists). The slogan "I am not a victim. I am a survivor," quoted in Fermaglich, is from a cancer commercial featuring cyclist Lance Armstrong.

46. Terrence Des Pres, *The Survivor: An Anatomy of Life in the Death Camps* (1976; New York: Oxford University Press, 1978), pp. 162–63.

47. B. F. Skinner, *Beyond Freedom and Dignity* (New York: Alfred A. Knopf, 1971), pp. 3, 138 (survival of mankind), 160, 19 ("traditional view"), 8–9 ("intentions, purposes"); Peter Caws, "Psychology without a Psyche," *New Republic* 165 (October 16, 1971): 33. By late October 1971 *Beyond Freedom and Dignity* had sold seventy-five thousand copies and was number five on one list of best-selling nonfiction books. William P. Blatty's *The Exorcist* was number two on the fiction list. Sidebar to Richard Sennett, review of *Beyond Freedom and Dignity*, *New York Times Book Review*, October 24, 1971.

48. Paul F. Boller Jr., "Conditional Man in a Behaviorist Universe," review of *Beyond Freedom and Dignity*, in *Southwest Review* 57 (Winter 1972): 82 ("sum total"); Sennett, in *New York Times Book Review*, p. 16 (Heisenberg); Spencer Klaw, "B. F. Skinner's Brave New World," *Natural History* 81 (January 1972): 86; Carl T. Rogers, "In Retrospect: Forty-Six Years," *American Psychologist* 29 (February 1974): 118 ("architect"); Herbert M. Lefcourt, "The Function of the Illusions of Control and Freedom," *American Psychologist* 28 (May 1973): 427, 424, 425 ("bedrock").

49. Rogers, "In Retrospect," p. 119 (elitist); George Kateb, "Toward a Wordless World," review of *Beyond Freedom and Dignity*, in *Atlantic Monthly* 228 (October 1971): 124 ("language of judgment"). The Rand reference is from Wikipedia, "Beyond Freedom and Dignity," http://en.wikipedia.org/wiki/Beyond_freedom_and_dignity; ISI's worst book list is at http://www.isi.org/journals/ir/50best_worst/50worst.html (both accessed 12 February 2008).

50. Cole, *Cult of True Victimhood*, pp. 11, 21 (books), 47 (Pfeiffer). Books in the antivictimist vein include Charles J. Sykes, *A Nation of Victims: The Decay of the American Character* (1992); Camille Paglia, *Sex, Art, and American Culture: Essays* (1992), which presents her controversial thoughts on rape; Robert Hughes, *Culture of Complaint: The Fraying of America* (1993); and Alan M. Dershowitz, *The Abuse Excuse: And Other Cop-Outs, Sob Stories, and Evasions of Responsibility* (1994).

51. Cole, *Cult of True Victimhood*, pp. 112–13.

52. Ibid., pp. 118, 126, 141, 133 ("personal responsibility"), 138 ("victim's journey").

53. On Lifton, see *Trial Transcript* (Lifton testimony), pp. 318–21. Carl N. Degler, *In Search of Human Nature: The Decline and Revival of Darwinism in American Social Thought* (New York: Oxford University Press, 1991), pp. 218–29.

54. Dr. Benjamin Spock, *Baby and Child Care* (1946; New York: Pocket Books/Wallaby, 1977), pp. 14–15; Gerhart Niemeyer, "Of Human Dignity," *National Review* 28 (April 2, 1976): 333.

55. Jonathan Haidt, *The Happiness Hypothesis: Finding Modern Truth in Ancient Wisdom* (New York: Basic Books, 2006), p. 17.

56. Killen, *1973 Nervous Breakdown*, p. 8.

57. Adapted from Graebner, "America's *Poseidon Adventure*."

58. Review of *Network*, in *Roger Ebert's Video Companion*, 1997 ed. (Kansas City: Andrews and McMeel, 1997), p. 539.

59. Graebner, "America's *Poseidon Adventure*," p. 173.

60. Des Pres, *Survivor*, pp. 151–62 (Elkins, Bettelheim), 6 ("defiance," "gesture"), 161 (suicide), 9 ("hardminded"), 21 (fearless), 106–8 (acts of resistance),

136 (gave and shared), 8 ("consent to death"), 29–49 (bear witness). Fort's discussion of Des Pres is in *Trial Transcript*, p. 441.

61. Des Pres, *Survivor*, pp. 13 ("simply a victim"), 7 ("decency intact," "soul"), 65–66 ("dignity," "selfhood").

62. *Quest/77* 1 (March–April 1977): "Prologue" and 98, 108. On the motorcycle boom of the 1970s—another example of risk behavior—see Melissa Holbrook Pierson, "Precious Dangers: The Lessons of the Motorcycle," *Harper's Magazine* 290 (May 1995): 69, 75, 78.

63. *Trial Transcript* (Hearst testimony), p. 261.

64. Daniel Lang, "A Reporter at Large: The Bank Drama," *New Yorker* 50 (November 25, 1974): 72 ("nice"), 92 (hips), 118, 78 (Ljungberg).

65. "The Trauma of Captivity," *Time* 114 (December 24, 1979): 59; Leo Eitinger, "The Effects of Captivity," in *Victims of Terrorism*, ed. Frank M. Ochberg and David A. Soskis (Boulder, CO: Westview Press, 1982), p. 78 ("family and the police"); Jared Tinklenberg, "Coping with Terrorist Victimization," in *Victims of Terrorism*, p. 64 ("identification"); David A. Soskis and Frank M. Ochberg, "Concepts of Terrorist Victimization," in *Victims of Terrorism*, pp. 123–24. On Elizabeth Smart, see Paul T. P. Wong, "Elizabeth Smart and the Stockholm Syndrome," accessible through http://www.meaning.ca/archives/all_articles.htm (accessed 12 February 2008).

66. Thomas Strentz, "The Stockholm Syndrome: Law Enforcement Policy and Hostage Behavior," in Ochberg and Soskis, *Victims of Terrorism*, p. 156 ("recapture them").

67. For Dean quotation, see Wikipedia, "Nixon Enemies List," http://en.wikipedia.org/wiki/Nixon_enemies_list (accessed 24 February 2006).

68. Chidester, *Salvation and Suicide*, pp. 142–43; McLellan and Avery, *Voices of Guns*, p. 260.

69. Stephen Paul Miller, *The Seventies Now: Culture as Surveillance* (Durham, NC: Duke University Press, 1999), pp. 80 ("everyday characters"), 84–86 (delegation of the law).

70. Timothy Melley, *Empire of Conspiracy: The Culture of Paranoia in Postwar America* (Ithaca: Cornell University Press, 2000), pp. 1–10.

71. Alexander, *Anyone's Daughter*, p. 189.

72. For Perry's view of the Kennedy assassination, see McLellan and Avery, *Voices of Guns*, pp. 175–76. See also Mark Fenster, *Conspiracy Theories: Secrecy and Power in American Culture* (Minneapolis: University of Minnesota Press, 1999).

73. Alexander, *Anyone's Daughter*, pp. 503–6; *Trial Transcript* (Bailey closing), p. 590.

74. Susan Jeffords, *Hard Bodies: Hollywood Masculinity in the Reagan Era* (New Brunswick, NJ: Rutgers University Press, 1994), pp. 1–13. On the attempt to achieve identity through bodily mutilation, see Kim Hewitt, *Mutilating the Body: Identity in Blood and Ink* (Bowling Green, OH: Bowling Green State University Popular Press, 1997), esp. pp. 20, 21–25, 60.

75. On the Boston busing controversy, see Ronald P. Formisano, *Boston against Busing: Race, Class, and Ethnicity in the 1960s and 1970s* (Chapel Hill: University of North Carolina Press, 1991). On family in the 1970s, see Carroll, *It Seemed Like Nothing Happened*, pp. 278–96.

76. On the turn from rehabilitation to retribution in the criminal justice system in the mid-1970s, see "Reappraisal of Prison Policy," in *Editorial Research Reports*, ed. Hoyt Gimlin, 1976 (Washington, D.C.: Congressional Quarterly, n.d.), 1:187–201, and Killen, *1973 Nervous Breakdown*, pp. 39–40.

77. Kenneth Cmiel, "The Politics of Civility," in *The Sixties: From Memory to History*, ed. David Farber (Chapel Hill: University of North Carolina Press, 1994), pp. 263–90.

78. Patrick Allitt, *Religion in America since 1945: A History* (New York: Columbia University Press, 2003), pp. 150–52; Walter H. Capps, *The New Religious Right: Piety, Patriotism, and Politics* (Columbia: University of South Carolina Press, 1990), p. 8 ("most often used words").

79. Editorial, *Richmond News Leader*, March 22, 1976, in *Editorials on File*, 7:466; editorial, *Winston-Salem* (NC) *Journal*, March 23, 1976, in *Editorials on File*, 7:464; Allitt, *Religion in America since 1945*, p. 157 ("secular humanism"); Erling Jorstad, *Popular Religion in America: The Evangelical Voice* (Westport, CT: Greenwood Press, 1993), p. 51.

80. Capps, *New Religious Right*, p. 27.

81. "The Yes, No and Maybe on Driver's Licenses," *New York Times*, 1 November 2007, p. A20; Marc Santora, "Immigration from Talking Point to Sore Point," *New York Times*, 1 November 2007, p. 1 ("seemed to defend it"); Jeff Zeleny and Michael Cooper, "Edwards Raises Criticism of Clinton over Iraq Plan," *New York Times*, 5 November 2007, p. A17 ("tell-the-truth"); Katharine Q. Seelye, "Obama Plays a Convincing Obama in Clinton-Mocking Skit," *New York Times*, 5 November 2007, p. A17.

82. "The Two Faces of Patty Hearst," *Chicago Sun-Times*, 21 September 1975, p. 5; editorial, *Winston-Salem Journal*, 23 March 1976, *Editorials on File*, 7:464; Jorstad, *Popular Religion in America*, p. 51.

83. Edward M. Griffin, "Patricia Hearst and Her Foremothers: The Captivity Fable in America," *Centennial Review* 36 (Spring 1992): 321.

84. The text of Nixon's address is at http://www.mekong.net/cambodia/nixon430.htm (accessed 2 November 2007).

85. The Springsteen lyrics are from the song "The Promised Land," on *Darkness on the Edge of Town* (1978); Gaynor's recording of "I Will Survive" appears on *Love Tracks* (1979). On power, see T. J. Jackson Lears, "The Concept of Cultural Hegemony: Problems and Possibilities," *American Historical Review* 90 (June 1985): 567–93 (Gramsci); Guy Debord, *Society of the Spectacle* (1967; Detroit: Black & Red, 1983); and Michel Foucault, *Discipline and Punish: The Birth of the Prison* (1975; New York: Vintage, 1979), which includes a chapter on the panopticon.

86. On Springsteen's existential perspective, see Graebner, "America's *Poseidon Adventure*," pp. 163–64. The lyric is from "Thunder Road" (1975).

87. Griffin, "Patricia Hearst and Her Foremothers," pp. 321 (Lawrence quotations), 322 ("bad captive").

88. "The Vanishing American Hero," *U.S. News & World Report* 79 (July 21, 1975): 16–18; J. H. Plumb, "Disappearing Heroes," *Horizon* 16 (Autumn 1974): 48–51; David Thomson, "The End of the American Hero," *Film Comment* 17 (July/August 1981): 13–17; "TV Actress Tops List of Students' Heroes," *Senior Scholastic* 109 (February 10, 1977): 15.

89. Killen, *1973 Nervous Breakdown*, pp. 96–103.

90. See Jeffords, *Hard Bodies*, pp. 34–41.

91. Philip Jenkins, *Decade of Nightmares: The End of the Sixties and the Making of Eighties America* (New York: Oxford University Press, 2006), p. 20.

92. Castiglia, *Bound and Determined*, pp. 98–99.

93. Thomas Frank, *What's the Matter with Kansas?: How Conservatives Won the Hearts of America* (New York: Henry Holt, 2004).

94. The cook's comment appeared in *Ladies Home Journal*. The story is told in Isenberg, "Not 'Anyone's Daughter,'" p. 650.

95. Richard Wightman Fox, *Trials of Intimacy: Love and Loss in the Beecher-Tilton Scandal* (Chicago: University of Chicago Press, 1999), pp. 3, 5, 294, 298, 309, 315; Michael Lienesch, *In the Beginning: Fundamentalism, the Scopes Trial, and the Making of the Antievolution Movement* (Chapel Hill: University of North Carolina Press, 2007), pp. 138, 144, 148, 150, 152, 155, 181, 182.

96. John W. Ward, "The Meaning of Lindbergh's Flight," *American Quarterly* 10 (Spring 1958): 3–16.

acknowledgments

Patty's Got a Gun emerged from a grant from the American Council of Learned Societies for a book on genetics and culture (you don't always get what you want), and I thank the Council for its support. I am grateful to Dianne Bennett, Casey Blake, and an anonymous reader for the University of Chicago Press for their careful and thoughtful critiques of earlier versions of the book. Joel Score's thorough, informed, and elegant copyediting improved the book immeasurably. A special thanks to my editor, Doug Mitchell, whose understanding of the project and ongoing enthusiasm for it have been invaluable (sometimes you get what you need).

William Graebner
Buffalo, New York
February 11, 2008

index

The abbreviation PH is used throughout the index for Patty Hearst. Italicized page numbers indicate illustrations.